# Global Perspectives on Graduate International Collaborations

## Proceedings of the 2009 Strategic Leaders Global Summit on Graduate Education

**December 5-6, 2009
San Francisco, California**

**COUNCIL OF GRADUATE SCHOOLS**

# Global Perspectives on Graduate International Collaborations

## Proceedings of the 2009 Strategic Leaders Global Summit on Graduate Education

Prepared for publication by: Julia D. Kent.

ISBN-13: 978-1-933042-28-2
ISBN-10: 1-933042-28-1

10  9  8  7  6  5  4  3  2  1        10  09  08

# TABLE OF CONTENTS

# CONTENTS

*Note: The names of co-authors who did not attend the summit appear at the top of the essay to which they contributed.*

# FOREWORD

The 2010 Strategic Leaders Global Summit in San Francisco, California gave focused attention to a topic that frequently emerged in the two previous annual summits: the role of international collaborations in supporting and enhancing the missions of universities worldwide. There is no doubt that collaborations such as joint and dual degree programs and research exchanges hold out enormous opportunities and benefits to graduate institutions, students and faculty, and that these benefits have already diffused into the global scholarship and research enterprise. Yet among graduate leaders, many questions remain about the best strategies for developing international collaborations and managing the risks associated with new international partnerships. Recognizing that not every institution will answer these questions in the same way, the participants in this year's Global Summit worked together to map a variety of issues shaping collaboration across their different international and institutional contexts. This volume reflects our collective efforts to analyze the variety of challenges we face, to learn from one another, and to build consensus around common values and priorities.

Debra W. Stewart
President
Council of Graduate Schools

# ACKNOWLEDGMENTS

**M**any groups and individuals contributed to the successful convening of the 2010 Global Summit. I would particularly like to thank the Summit Steering Committee for its guidance on the development of the summit agenda, and the 2010 summit delegates for their thoughtful contributions to the forum and this volume.

I would also like to recognize the CGS staff members who made this publication possible: Julia Kent, who edited this manuscript; Daniel Denecke, who played a key role in developing the summit theme and agenda; Eleanor Babco, who brought her expertise in overseeing CGS summits to the organization of the 2010 convening; and Joshua Mahler, who helped edit and design the summit materials.

The San Francisco Global Summit was made possible with a generous gift from ProQuest, the official publisher of U.S. dissertations. On behalf of the Council of Graduate Schools, I would like to thank them for recognizing the importance of graduate international collaborations and for their ongoing support of graduate education and research.

Debra W. Stewart
President
Council of Graduate Schools

# I. INTRODUCTION: GRADUATE INTERNATIONAL COLLABORATIONS

The 2009 Strategic Leaders Global Summit built upon the outcomes of two highly successful global convenings. The first Global Summit, which took place in Banff in 2007, established a set of principles and priorities to guide future collaboration among graduate leaders worldwide, and called for future summits on international issues in graduate education. In 2008, a second summit in Florence, Italy focused on the issue of scholarly integrity and research ethics in a global context, addressing the international legal frameworks that regulate international research, but also closely examining the procedures that support research ethics education and training. This year's summit gave focused attention to a topic that repeatedly emerged in these earlier meetings: the need for a strategic and coordinated approach to the wide range of international partnerships involving graduate institutions worldwide. Growing in number every year, these partnerships require careful definition and clarification both nationally and internationally. Graduate leaders must understand the complexity of the issues involved and give close attention to questions of quality and sustainability.

The purpose of the 2009 Global Summit was to share expertise on the wide range of issues shaping international collaborations in our various national, regional, and institutional contexts with the aim of developing promising or best practices in this area; the practical nature of this workshop is suggested by its title, *Graduate International Collaborations: How to Build and Sustain Them*. As in the past, we benefited from the contributions of a diverse group of national and regional experts, who this year represented Australia, Belgium, Canada, China, France, South Korea, the Middle East, the UK, and the US.

At the outset we established a set of goals in an effort to build common ground for ongoing conversation:

- Establish a clearer understanding of national and regional institutional procedures affecting transnational collaborations, as well as the constraints and opportunities that are emerging within them.
- Share strategies for achieving quality, compatibility, and sustainability.

- Build consensus around the core characteristics of effective joint and dual degree programs.
- Articulate effective next steps for shaping and refining institutional best practices.
- Outline possible methods for measuring the outcomes of collaborations of various types.

As we learned through the two previous summits, it is helpful to begin with a survey of the various national and regional frameworks that shape our topic. For panel one, presenters considered types of collaboration that exist in their national contexts, the value of these collaborations, and the role of government in creating and maintaining them. This broad view formed the foundation for the next panels by illuminating major differences between national contexts, as well as areas of common interest.

In panels two, three, and four, presenters addressed, from both national and institutional perspectives, a wide range of issues they have observed and confronted throughout the collaboration process. While many of the questions organizing these sessions were broad in scope—"Why collaborate in the first place?" or "What are the benefits of collaborations to various groups within the university?"— these presentations were built upon the very specific experiences of the experts assembled. The insights exchanged in these earlier forums paved the way for a broader discussion, in panel five, of global networks that support international collaborations, including strong models and best practice research.

The final step in the 2009 Global Summit was a session in which the entire group of participants contributed to a set of consensus points and plans for future work, a concrete document that clarified the outcomes and conclusions of the summit. These "Principles and Practices for Effective International Collaborations" promise to provide graduate deans and other senior university leaders with a strong starting point for managing existing collaborations and developing new ones.[1]

In conclusion, I would like to express my deep gratitude to ProQuest UMI for generously sponsoring the 2009 summit. Without their support, it would not have been possible to establish the Strategic Leaders Summit on Graduate Education as an ongoing dialogue. I would also like to thank the international steering committee who helped create and approve the summit agenda, as well as each participant at this year's meeting. I am confident that our efforts as both individuals and as a group will expand the international discussion of

---

[1] See Appendix A.

graduate international collaborations. This volume of proceedings will serve as an invaluable resource for many graduate communities worldwide.

Debra W. Stewart
President
Council of Graduate Schools

# II. NATIONAL AND REGIONAL PERSPECTIVES ON GRADUATE INTERNATIONAL COLLABORATIONS

## Summary of Presentations and Group Discussion

For participants in the 2010 Global Summit, graduate international collaborations conjured many different mental images. Many referenced a concept described by CGS Annual Meeting speaker AnnaLee Saxenian—"brain circulation"—in which knowledge flows freely across national borders via individuals with ties to multiple national research networks.[1] **Karen DePauw** (Virginia Tech) commented that joint and dual degree programs brought to mind "arrows going to and from universities across some pond," and reminded other participants that other models were possible, such as consortia representing multiple arrows traveling in different directions. Yet another striking idea emerged in a paper by **Allison Sekuler** (McMaster University), who figuratively described a global collaboration as an international "committee" of talented individuals working together to solve the world's most daunting research challenges.[2] These creative descriptions reflect the fact that leaders in graduate education are imagining new circuits and concepts of international partnership and exchange, as well as new global networks of graduate students and faculty.

While the international climate of research and education leads us to imagine a world with more permeable national boundaries, national contexts do still pose constraints and shape opportunities for international collaboration. It was therefore helpful to begin a discussion of international collaboration with a survey of the national environments in which institutional partnerships are formed. The opening session of the Global Summit was designed to examine differences between the national (and in some cases, regional) frameworks that define the priorities and structures of collaboration and to address differences in definitions of terms that may be taken for granted in one's national context.

---

1    AnnaLee Saxenian, *From Brain Drain to Brain Circulation: Rethinking the Global Knowledge Economy*. Plenary presentation at CGS Annual Meeting, December 4, 2009, www.cgsnet.org/portals/0/pdf/am09_Saxenian.pdf

2    See Allison Sekuler's essay, "International Collaboration and Capacity-Building: Creating Davincis-by-Committee," pp. 113-17.

Presenters for this opening panel addressed questions such as,

- What forms of collaboration exist in your country or region, and why are they valued?
- What role does federal, state, or provincial government play in the process of creating and maintaining collaborations in graduate education and research?
- What are the specific legal and ethical issues affecting these collaborations? (For example, in research, what issues surround copyright and intellectual property laws and the responsible conduct of research, and in education, what are the issues affecting diploma "seals" or "badges?")
- What are the most pressing issues and questions affecting past and future graduate international collaborations at universities in your country? What are your greatest obstacles and opportunities?

Presentations from participants representing Australia, Canada, France and the European Union, South Korea, the United Arab Emirates, and the United States, provided a reminder that challenges of graduate international collaborations for universities will vary widely by country, as will some of the current approaches to solving them. Because of the diversity of the presentations, the summaries of panel presentations have been organized into the three topics below.

## The Role of Governments

Panel presentations underscored important differences in the roles played by federal, state, and provincial governments in shaping universities' decisions about which types of collaborations to pursue and fund. Details about the role of governments in shaping institutional partnerships helped participants take note of the fact that university leaders in different countries may be referring to different organizational structures when discussing "top-down" versus "bottom-up" collaborations. In countries where the Ministry of Education plays a major role in higher education, for example, the federal government sets a strong agenda for strategic decision-making about international education and research training. State and provincial governments may also play a strong role as well. **Carolyn Watters** (Dalhousie University) noted that in Canada, provincial governments fund educational institutions and may set limits on tuition, while federal governments play a direct role in defining the national research agenda.

Panelists also demonstrated that "top-down" strategy may include different regional stakeholders and authorities. Two examples of such regional networks came from Europe and Asia. **Jean Chambaz** (Université Pierre et Marie Curie) explained that in Europe, the Bologna reforms have sought to increase the mobility of researchers throughout Europe, while the Salzburg initiatives have helped define the European doctorate as a degree that requires international research. National university systems are increasingly working together to meet the European agenda for mobility and international research experience within the doctorate. Describing what he referred to as "an Asian version of the Erasmus project in Europe," **Kyung Chan Min** (Yonsei University) said that in the South Korea, the Ministry of Education and Science and Technology supports a "Campus Asia" project with China and Japan. The "top" may not only include one's national government, but also larger regional bodies seeking to create a complementary agenda for international higher education.

Despite these differences in the level and type of authorities involved in strategic decision-making, participants agreed that it is crucial for collaboration to be driven and supported by faculty research interests and relationships. The role of university leaders in creating such an environment for faculty, regardless of the national and regional differences among governments, was directly addressed in panels two and three.

## Common Challenges

Despite the differences outlined above, presenters for the introductory panel also outlined a number of common challenges faced by governments, university leaders, and other stakeholders in developing strong and sustainable university-to-university partnerships. The first of these challenges was ensuring quality in the face of ambitious agendas for the internationalization of graduate education and research. Describing the higher education landscape in the United Arab Emirates, for example, **Chet Jablonski** (Zayed University) said that the 38-year-old, resource-rich country must find ways to "harness" the rapid growth of higher education, which is currently dominated by models imported from the United States. Addressing a very different and older higher education system, but one nevertheless pursuing rapid changes in the nature of graduate education, **Dr. Chambaz** said that European universities must work to ensure that they carefully respond to a goal set out by the European Ministers for Higher Education: to ensure that 20% of graduates will have engaged in some form of mobility by 2020. Mobility for the sake of mobility will not be enough; it must be mobility that productively supports doctoral students and their careers.

A second set of challenges related to significant differences in funding structures supporting graduate institutions in different countries, which often make it difficult for universities to develop agreements about the terms of student and faculty exchange. **Dr. DePauw** outlined a number of the specific areas that need closer attention: for students, agreements about tuition, stipends, and assistantships, as well as funding for health insurance, housing, program fees, and living expenses; and for faculty, compensation and other benefits.

A third challenge concerned the legal and regulatory structures governing research. **Maxwell King** (Monash University) outlined intellectual property as a topic of particular concern. Both **Dr. King** and **Dr. DePauw** also indicated that international collaborations tend to raise significant issues about research ethics and the responsible conduct of research in different countries, and **Dr. DePauw** proposed that this issue be addressed in later sessions.[3]

## Shared Benefits

All of the presenters for panel one shed light on the benefits of graduate international collaborations to their regions, countries, and the international research enterprise of which they are a part. Throughout the discussion period, many participants referenced the CGS Annual Meeting presentation by global innovation expert John Kao, who argues that that the world's most "wicked problems," or those that pose the greatest threat to the environment, health and security, must be solved by drawing upon a larger pool of global talent and creativity. Because all countries have a social and economic stake in solving these problems, participants noted, it is essential to prepare students and faculty from all countries to confront research questions that are international in scope. As **Dr. King** observed in his presentation, it is also important to consider the measurable outcomes of collaborations, and he cited growing evidence that international collaborations produce research publications that have a greater and broader global impact.

Overall, the opening session of the Global Summit was important both in content and process. The information provided in the individual presentations allowed participants to compare their differences and to test perceptions of national differences against substantive facts and data. The panel also affirmed

---

3  For a discussion of this topic, see Sheila Bonde's essay, "Preparing Students for Supervised Research in an International Context: Etiquette and Ethics," pp. 84-6.

one of the values underlying this and all of the previous summits, the growing need for graduate leaders to better understand common values as they work toward developing international priorities and best practices for graduate education and research.

# Canadian Perspectives on Graduate International Collaborations

## Carolyn Watters
## Dalhousie University

## Regional Experience: Atlantic Canada

The Atlantic region of Canada includes four small provinces (Nova Scotia, New Brunswick, Prince Edward Island, and Newfoundland and Labrador) with a population of under three million people and roughly 10,000 graduate students. In this context, it is not surprising that regional collaborations are frequent and sought after. For example, there is considerable cross-university supervision and committee membership at both the Master's and PhD levels. There are degree programs shared by universities, such as the Master's in Health Administration Research and the universities have participated in a shared website that lists all graduate programs offered in the region. Three of the provinces share a common regulatory body, the Maritime Provinces Higher Education Commission, that reviews all new graduate programs in the region. In addition to national level connections with CAGS (Canadian Association of Graduate Studies) and North American connections through CGS, the Atlantic universities network extensively at the graduate level with universities in the eastern parts of Ontario and with Quebec and the northeastern states through Northeastern Association of Graduate Schools (NAGS).

At the regional level, difficulties in collaboration arise where university competition, especially for research dollars and graduate students, becomes an issue. At the same time, regional similarities make research and program collaborations attractive. One component of this collaboration is networking regionally for partnership in large national research networks. These regional initiatives often require that universities deal with substantive graduate issues such as intellectual property, appeals, admission/dismissal regulations, joint degrees, transfer of credit, and standards of ethics review of proposed research.

At the regional level, the provincial governments can support or can undermine efforts by universities to collaborate at the graduate level. This is true not only regionally, but also nationally, and internationally. In particular, provincial governments in the Atlantic provinces can increase commitments to graduate student funding, support for joint programs, and support for engagement in national network research opportunities.

## National Collaborations

In Canada, education falls under the provincial jurisdiction. This means that provinces have responsibility for funding educational institutions, and often for imposing limits to tuition. At the same time, the federal government has responsibility for manpower and for the national research agenda. For example, the large research councils (NSERC, natural sciences and engineering, SSHRC, social sciences and humanities, and CIHR, health research) provide graduate student scholarships and research grants that are federally funded and federally regulated. The Canadian government supports graduate initiatives both nationally and internationally, directly through scholarships to students and indirectly through grants to researchers and research networks. In Canada a higher proportion of research is carried out in the universities than in the U.S. It is the federal government that provides the vast majority of funding for graduate students and it is the federal government that establishes the areas of research focus for research funding. Programs to increase study abroad for graduate students and to develop professional skills also come from the federal level. Less directly, an important role of the Canadian government and its agencies is to bring in national level organizations such as the Association of Universities and Colleges of Canada, Canadian Association of Graduate Schools, Federation of Social Sciences and Humanities, and the Canadian Alliance of Student Associations, for broad participation in policy discussions related to graduate education and research both in Canada and internationally.

Partly because of the way in which the population is spread across Canada and the country's relatively small population, Canadian researchers actively engage in research collaborations involving graduate students. This participatory collaborative model supported by initiatives at the provincial and national level within Canada provides the foundation for building international collaborations that open up new opportunities for participation in the design and delivery of innovative programs to extend the impact of the talent in our relatively smaller institutions, and to build international networks to support the next generation of graduate education.

# Graduate Education and International Collaborations: The Australian Context

## Maxwell King
## Monash University

## 1. Forms of Collaboration in Australia

A number of Australian universities have branch campuses in other countries; mine (Monash University) has campuses in Malaysia and South Africa. We also have a joint venture Research Institute in India with the Indian Institute of Technology Bombay (IITB). A high proportion of Australian universities have doctoral students in jointly awarded degree programs with institutions in other countries. International Research collaborations are becoming more common – they are encouraged through our centrally awarded research grant systems (Australian Research Council and National Medical Health and Research Council). Monash requires there to be an existing research collaboration before it will approve a jointly awarded degree. While research collaborations are more common between Australian universities, there are difficulties in setting up jointly awarded degrees between Australian universities. We are hoping the current government will overcome this problem.

## 2. The Value of Such Collaborations

There is evidence that research collaborations across institutions and across countries lead to research publications with, on average, greater impact than is otherwise the case. We therefore value such collaborations and students can be the glue that helps make them work. We also get access to high quality students. Some of these will be research leaders of the future and hopefully their exposure to an Australian university (and Australia) will have positive spin-offs for future collaborations. We are facing a likely shortage of researchers in the future, particularly research leaders. Many of our international research students stay on in Australia after graduation or come back to Australia after returning home.

## 3. The Role of Government

The current Australian Government is talking a great deal about the importance of research collaboration and has introduced funding schemes that encourage domestic collaboration. Many graduate deans feel there is more to be done. The government also have (limited) scholarship schemes for collaboration in doctoral training and allow degree completions of jointly awarded degrees to count equally with normal degree completions in the formula for government block funding for research degree places. This does provide an incentive for jointly awarded degree programs.

## 4.   Legal and Ethical Issues

Agreement on intellectual property rights/obligations is the biggest problem affecting collaborations. There are also difficulties with ethical requirements/ rules differing from institution to institution and country to country. So far this has not been a great problem but I suspect one day we will have our first case of research misconduct. At Monash, student insurance and student visas have been issues for our IITB-Monash Ph.D. program.

# Graduate International Collaborations in South Korea

## Kyung Chan Min
## Yonsei University

## What forms of collaboration exist in your country and/or region?

Most universities in Korea have been establishing various types of partnerships with many other universities in foreign countries. For example, Yonsei University has established partnerships so far with 578 universities in 59 countries. The number of students at Yonsei University is now about 37,000, including 11,000 graduate students. In addition to exchange programs, universities are developing various models related to joint or dual/double degree programs at the graduate level. For example, Yonsei University participates in the Yonsei-Keio-Fudan triangular education system in which the three universities, located in Korea, Japan and China, promote close research and education relationships such as student exchange, research collaboration and seminars. For this successful program, every semester we offer a couple of lectures simultaneously in three campuses using a real-time distance learning system.

## What is the value of such collaborations to your country and/or region?

At present, globalization drives the recent efforts of Korean universities to increase their status in the international community in terms of the quality of education and research as well as in university rankings. Many universities are very actively working to expand their networks with other universities in foreign countries. The international collaboration system helps the participating universities understand each other better, and better understanding facilitates more collaboration. Through this cyclical system, the region can establish a robust academic network.

## What role does government play in the process of creating and maintaining collaborations in graduate education and research?

Recently the Ministry of Education and Science & Technology has established the Graduate School Support Division. This means that the government has a strong will to support graduate schools in many aspects. As an effort by the government, the Ministry of Education and Science and Technology of Korea is promoting the "Campus Asia" Project with China and Japan in order to accelerate regional cooperation, and this initiative might be seen as an Asian version of Erasmus project in Europe.

In addition, The National Institute for International Education Development (NIIED), established by the Ministry of Education and Science and Technology in 1992, promotes international exchange and cooperation programs. One of the most important activities of NIIED is inviting and managing Korean government scholarship students, which total approximately 1,100 students from 87 countries at the undergraduate and graduate level.

Also, the Korea Foundation, established by the Ministry of Foreign Affairs, actively promotes exchange programs to study in Korea, inviting young next-generation leaders who are expected to play vital roles in their respective specialized areas in the global community of the 21st century. The Foundation supports the establishment of Korean Studies and Korean language professorships at overseas universities that have demonstrated a strong commitment to the field.

Furthermore, the Graduate Studies Fellowship Program is designed to assist talented foreign graduate students in Korean Studies with scholarships for their coursework and/or research. The Postdoctoral Fellowship Program provides promising and highly qualified recent Ph.D. recipients with the opportunity to conduct research in the field of Korean studies at leading universities.

## What are the specific legal and ethical issues affecting these collaborations?

It seems to me that there are no serious legal issues in the development of international collaborations except for Intellectual Property (IP). The IP issue must be carefully considered and actively discussed among partners at the government level as well as at the university or individual level.

## What are the most pressing issues and questions affecting past and future graduate international collaborations at universities in your country?

As far as incoming students are concerned, the most pressing issues are how to evaluate the quality of foreign students during the admissions procedure, and how to provide a comfortable environment for foreign scholars and students and their families in terms of financial support, living conditions, education, culture, etc.

For outgoing students, the issues arise in the details of exchange programs, and include matters such as reciprocal requirements on numbers of students and the tuition fees for exchange students, and the regional imbalances within international cooperation agreements. In fact, international collaboration is generally concentrated on the North American region—particularly with U.S. universities.

## What are your greatest obstacles and opportunities?

One of our greatest obstacles is language barriers. In many cases, international students have difficulties both in English and Korean. At present, 30% of lectures are taught in English. Other obstacles are insufficient resources, inertia within university administrations, government regulations, precedents, and the frequent turnover of administrative leadership, which lead to the halting of projects or changes in policy.

Graduate international collaborations are a great opportunity for students and researchers, introducing them to a whole new world and training environment that prepares them for new challenges in their academic career and research, if they are ready. Students and researchers are now living in a time of "brain circulation," to refer to the term used by AnnaLee Saxenian in her presentation at the CGS meeting, or a time of fluid global networks of knowledge.[1]

---

1    AnnaLee Saxenian, *From Brain Drain to Brain Circulation: Rethinking the Global Knowledge Economy*.  Plenary presentation at CGS Annual Meeting, December 4, 2009. www.cgsnet.org/portals/0/pdf/am09_Saxenian.pdf

*Global Perspectives on Graduate International Collaborations*          **15**

# European Perspectives on Doctoral International Collaborations

## Jean Chambaz
## Université Pierre et Marie Curie

Through the last decade, the development of collaborations between European universities has been an important driver for the creation of a European Higher Education Area (EHEA). Through the Bologna process, higher education has been modernized, leading to greater compatibility and comparability, and its international profile has been raised considerably.

The future, as outlined by the Leuven Communiqué adopted by the European ministers for higher education in April this year, contains a number of challenges, among which mobility is proclaimed as the hallmark of European higher education. *"Within each of the three cycles, opportunities for mobility shall be created in the structure of degree programmes. [...] Mobility of students, early stage researchers and staff enhances the quality of programmes and excellence in research; it strengthens the academic and cultural internationalization of European higher education. Important for personal development and employability, it fosters respect for diversity and a capacity to deal with other cultures."*[1] The communiqué even sets for 2020 the target that 20% of those graduating should have experienced mobility while also calling for more diverse types of mobility with a broader scope.

Doctoral education has been part of the Bologna process, as the third cycle, from the 2003 Berlin Communiqué. In this framework, based on an intensive bottom-up work from European universities developed under the auspices of EUA (2004-2005), the Salzburg principles drew up in 2005 the new vision of doctoral education in Europe. They were largely endorsed by hundreds of European universities from the Nice conference (2006) as well as by the Council of European Ministers in charge of Higher Education (Bergen 2005, London 2007) and the European Commission.

*"Beyond doubt, a quiet revolution is under way in doctoral education"*[2] in Europe, and European universities have been at the forefront of these reforms. EUA's evidence on the rapid growth of structured doctoral programmes is that schools now offer greater critical mass, better supervision and enhanced

---

1    The Bologna Process 2020: The European Higher education Area in the new decade. Communiqué of the Conference of European Ministers Responsible for Higher Education, Leuven and Louvain la Neuve, 28-29 April 2009.

2    John Smith, in *Research Europe*, 25 June 2009.

employment opportunities for PhDs in both public and private sectors. Another sign is the success of the EUA Council for Doctoral Education. In less than two years, more than 160 universities have joined the council. It is their forum for sharing promising practice, information and data, building European collaboration among doctoral and graduate schools, and creating exchange mechanisms and mobility for PhD candidates and university staff.

Far from a uniform standardized model, the Salzburg principles set a common framework and a common goal to reach by different routes. Their implementation by most universities throughout Europe in very diverse contexts demonstrates their strength, accuracy and operability and accumulates a considerable amount of original experiences and innovative practices that enrich this new vision. However, there is a risk that the local nature of the reforms makes them less visible for the non-university stakeholders and decision-makers at both the national and European level. The next year will be characterized by the CDE revisiting the Salzburg principles five years after they were launched. The goal for the **Salzburg II initiative** will not be a new set of principles, but rather an affirmation of the "spirit of Salzburg" through consultation with the members on the most important, concrete issues. It is central to Salzburg II to emphasize that the principles rest upon the vast know-how of European universities and to stress the need for bottom-up implementation.

The Salzburg principles stressed the specificity of the doctorate as the degree in which learning is achieved through the practice of an original research project, bridging by that means the EHEA and the European Research Area (ERA). If this basis is compromised, the doctorate as such will lose its value. For this reason, it is by nature different from the first and second cycles. As a consequence, the format and assessment tools developed through the Bologna process for the two first cycles are not appropriate at the doctoral level. Reform of doctoral education cannot be reduced to the introduction of more taught elements, credit systems or skills provision. These are all secondary to the development of a dynamic research environment in which the doctoral candidates take part as early stage researchers. This is highly connected to the development of the ERA, and the formation of researchers should be an explicit part of the individual ERA initiatives. The structuring of doctoral education deals mostly with the means of achieving a critical mass within the research environment and the means of exposing doctoral candidates ("PhD students," "early stage researchers") to a wide range of opportunities to develop their creativity, their autonomy, and their personal and professional skills in order to be prepared for careers in R&D as well as in any other sector.

The specificity of the doctoral level is particularly illustrated in relation to the mobility issue. In the first and second cycles, mobility deals with cohorts of students and matching learning outcomes and curricula. At the doctoral level it must be based on genuine research and take into account the highly individual trajectories of candidates. Mobility should not be an end in itself. Because good research is by nature international, the international agenda is a key part, of any research environment. Furthermore, the global problems we face (e.g., climate change, energy, healthcare and security) need global solutions and these in turn will require global brain power and new multidisciplinary approaches.

Thus universities offer different opportunities to their doctoral candidates to answer different specific needs and objectives.

International experience could be the first benefit gained through the participation of international students in doctoral programmes, while respecting a balance (some universities recruit more than 50% international students). Collaborative and joint doctoral programmes offer the doctoral candidate an invaluable opportunity to gain international experience in the context of their own research. There are two main types of programmes—collaborative, where the home institution awards the degree, and joint, where the successful candidate receives a single certificate jointly awarded by both host and home university. A half-way arrangement is the double degree, where two separate certificates are issued—although concerns are raised in this case about the risk of 'double-counting' of the PhD qualification.

The success of such initiatives depends on the combination of an existing genuine research-based collaboration or network; the identification of champions on both sides willing to carry out  the project and insitutional recognition for their role; full and continuous support by the top management of the institution; the need to be flexible in the planning and timing of visits in order to fit with the flow and needs of the doctoral research project. Additional issues include programme management, monitoring of progress, quality assurance, pastoral care and financial issues.

In addition, some universities are offering their doctoral candidates experiential learning in global skills as a component of their transferable skills programmes. For example, multinational residential skills workshops can be set up to cover a range of skills, but also include time to address intercultural as well as interdisciplinary differences–the latter sometimes being more potent than the former. These work best where the universities involved already have good interactions either as members of a consortium or as partners in collaborative/joint doctoral programmes.

It is critical that both institutions and funding bodies be aware of the full costs of international co-operations. Non-HEI stakeholders such as national governments, the European Commission and funding bodies need to be aware of legal and economic obstacles to creating good research environments as well as constructive ways to support such environments. Rigid legal frameworks concerning doctoral education should be reviewed in the light of improved transparency and accountability. Legal barriers to joint or dual degrees should, for example, be made more flexible to facilitate institutional co-operation. Mobility needs to be undergirded by social rights that are compatible with mobile careers.

Should we be optimistic reading the very challenging objectives the European ministers set to their own governments? *"Mobility shall be based on a range of practical measures pertaining to the funding of mobility, recognition, available infrastructure, visa and work permit regulations. Flexible study paths and active information policies, full recognition of study achievements, and the full portability of grants and loans are necessary requirements."*[3] Yes, if certain criteria are met.

Finally, there are many different models of international collaboration, each offering different opportunities to the developing researcher. Further discussion and sharing of ideas on these existing programmes and on potential new innovative programmes is needed.

Considering all the requirements listed above, the key to success is for institutions to focus on a limited number of strategically selected programmes and actions, rather than collecting non-active Memoranda of Understanding.

---

3    Leuven Communiqué

# International Partnerships in Graduate Education: A View from the United Arab Emirates

## Chet Jablonski
## Zayed University

## Background

Compared globally, graduate education in the UAE is a fledgling enterprise dominated by the importation of established models and partnerships, predominantly from the US. To put that statement in context, consider that the UAE, a federation of seven Emirates of very different means, is itself barely 38 years old, that Nationals make up only 19% of the total population of approximately 6 million, that the UAE as a whole is a "have" nation (subsequent to oil production in 1962), that cultural, religious and social drivers are at play, that it is a very young nation (50% of Nationals are under 20 years old) and that its leaders place an extremely high value on tertiary education "… that serves the needs of the nation." An interesting statistic is that the UAE has one of the highest post-secondary education participation rates in the world, with 95% of all females and 80% of all males who are enrolled in the final year of secondary school applying for admission to a higher education institution in the UAE or for study abroad. Given the federal policy to Emiratize the public service, an initiative that will require personnel trained at the post-graduate level, it is reasonable to expect a sustained high demand for Master's programming by Nationals, especially for women who are under-represented in the workforce. Under the guidance of the Minister of Higher Education and Scientific Research, Sheikh Nahyan bin Mubarak Al Nahyan, the UAE has moved quickly to improve its post-secondary system and has invested heavily, not only in the development of its three national institutions, the United Arab Emirates University (UAEU, established in 1977 in Al Ain), Higher Colleges of Technology (HCT, established in 1988 to provide technical training with campuses in 5 of the 7 Emirates) and the newest national university, Zayed (ZU, founded in 1998 with a mandate to educate national women and prepare them to actively participate in society), but has strengthened its post-secondary capabilities by encouraging the development of a number of private institutions, now totaling almost 60, based on varying blends of a public-private funding model. Baccalaureate level education and technical training at the three national institutions are available free to Emirati students, but tuition, with no difference between national and international students, is required for Master's programs in the three national institutions and the privates. It will not be news to anyone at this table that the UAE's position as a resource-rich state has resulted in unimaginably rapid change and that harnessing that change to derive maximum benefit for the country has been and will remain a challenge.

Many of the private institutions, which are located all over the UAE but particularly in Dubai and Abu Dhabi, are essentially branch campuses of their established parent US institutions. Private colleges and universities may be licensed by the Ministry of Higher Education and Scientific Research (MHESR); the number of licensed colleges and universities licensed has increased from 5 in 1997 to about 58 in 2009. English is the common standard language of instruction and faculty are almost exclusively expats, trained in the US, UK, Canada, Australia, New Zealand and, to a lesser extent EU countries. Not all such institutions, especially those located in academic free zones such as Dubai Academic City ("store front" operations of some 32 universities) or "Knowledge Village," pursue a UAE license. Free zone located institutions normally pay full costs of lease. These free zones offer "... 100% foreign ownership, 100% TAX free, 100% repatriation of assets and profits and effortless licensing, registration and government services."

Including the three national institutions, approximately 40 universities offer graduate programs at the Master's level. The focus of post-secondary education is to serve the needs of the nation and graduate programs are particularly heavily weighted in course-route (taught) professional Master's degrees in business, health education, public administration, IT etc. and complemented by a smaller number of research Master's programs in the sciences and engineering. Programs in the social sciences and humanities are generally under-represented. Some institutions, including UAEU, plan to offer doctoral programs.

As with education in general, there has been a heavy reliance on expat consultants and a highly trained resident expat population to fill key public and private sector positions. While government has always sent a steady stream of Nationals, mostly to the UK and US for post-secondary study abroad, today there is realization that government must take control of its own agenda and "Emiratize" the public sector. Emiratization, including provision of graduate education opportunities for Emirati women, many of whom find it difficult to travel outside the UAE, will couple with expat needs to assure continuing demand for Master's level training in the UAE.

## Models for Collaborative Graduate Education in the UAE

*Branch campus or "franchise university"*
The UAE welcomes the establishment of private branch campus institutions offering graduate programs and has set up tax free education free zones. There are caveats including very significant start-up costs (bricks and mortar), unpredictable enrollments, issues involving accreditation and the equivalence of degrees with the parent institution, sustained provision of faculty from the parent institution, and quality delivery and adaption of courses to local conditions. Quality issues aside, supply exceeds demand, especially in Dubai. This form of collaboration requires very significant up-front investment by the parent institution with a low expectation for short-term returns. Properly done, it's a "win-win" project (UAE builds capacity and knowledge capital; the parent institution extends influence). The graduate degree is normally equivalent to that of the host institution. Some potentially successful examples include:

1. Michigan State University Dubai (200 students, 20 staff situated in the Dubai Knowledge Village educational free zone which currently houses over 20 post secondary institutions) offering Bachelor's and Master's degree programs to Nationals and expats that are accredited and "equivalent to those offered by Michigan State University in the United States."[1]

2. Paris-Sorbonne University—Abu Dhabi. Follows Bologna 3+2 protocol and will offer (subject to enrollment minimums) 2 year master's degrees and (eventually PhD) delivered in French that will be acceptable in the European Higher Education Area. This initiative is funded by the Abu Dhabi Education Council ($323 million) and will result in a 23-acre campus on Al Reem Island development site.

3. Other likely successes in Abu Dhabi based on similar models include NYU's Abu Dhabi expansion (a comprehensive, residential liberal-arts and sciences branch campus, first intake 2010) and INSEAD, the elite French business school based in Fontainebleau, funded by the Abu Dhabi Education Council (ADEC) and scheduled to open in 2011.

4. "American University" franchises. The American University of Sharjha and the American University of Dubai are licensed and accredited in the US, offer quality undergraduate and graduate

---

1    Michigan State University Dubai Webpage, http://dubai.msu.edu/quick-facts/about-msu-dubai.

programming and receive financial support for the respective Emirate. AUS offers both professional and research Master's programs.

Branch campuses that have encountered major challenges:

1. George Mason University in Ras al Khaymah was closed in 2005 due to lack of funding from its UAE Emirate of Ras al Khaymah backers.
2. A number of Dubai-based institutions which do not receive UAE funding will likely find it difficult to survive – this list is very likely a long one.

*Partner Institution*

In this mode of collaboration, an international institution enters into a partnership with a local host institution. The partnership offers a range of knowledge transfer from full programs to supply of specific courses. Normally, the degree is awarded by the host UAE institution.

1. Masdar Institute of Technology (MIST, 22 faculty, first cohort of 99 students, 22 from UAE, admitted in fall 2009 with full fellowships, enrolled in 5 research Master's programs), a not-for-profit, independent, research-driven graduate institute developed with the cooperation of MIT and the Abu Dhabi Education Council (ADEC) and located in Masdar City, a $22-million zero carbon emission demonstration city being built at the edge of Abu Dhabi. "The Institute offers Master's and (eventually) PhD programs in science and engineering disciplines, with a focus on advanced energy and sustainable technologies."[2] The program will be delivered by MIT faculty on rotation form the parent campus. The degrees offered will not be from the parent MIT.
2. Zayed University offers a number of part-time professional, course-route Master's programs, most of which are partially taught by an international partner. For example, the Executive Master's in Health Care Administration is taught in partnership with University of Houston-Clear Lake and the University of North Carolina at Chapel Hill. The EMBA program is delivered in partnership with Clemson University and Oklahoma State University. The degree offered is from Zayed. Courses are delivered part-time in a cohort

---

2   Masdar Institute of Science and Technology Webpage, www.masdar.ac.ae/Menu/Index.aspx?Menu ID=37&CatID=74&mnu=Cat.

model using a hybrid distance/face-to-face delivery to minimize time away from the work place.

*Dual Degree*
In this variation, which requires a more fully developed "two-way" partnership, students complete part of the program at the host institution and part at the parent partner institution. The degree is issued by both partners. Although a dual degree offers many advantages to the students (two degrees, the ability to take courses at the parent institution, etc.), examples are scarce since, amongst other things, it is normally difficult to finds ways for students from the international partner to complete courses in the UAE.

Abu Dhabi University offers the only dual degree in the UAE. The Master's of Business Administration & Master's in International Business is a dual degree with ENPC-Paris. Students opting to take the dual degree must complete additional courses (6 in addition to the required 11) some of which are taught in Abu Dhabi by ENPC-Paris or on-line.

Taken together, these collaborations have served not only to globalize and strengthen postsecondary education in the UAE but also to privatize it.

# Views from the U.S. on Graduate International Collaborations

## Karen P. DePauw
## Virginia Tech

International partnerships and collaborations for graduate education vary around the United States and vary across universities as well. The broader region of North America presents even more diversity in approach to global graduate education when including Canada and Mexico. This paper will focus on a United States perspective.

Increasingly, universities have embraced internationalization and are encouraging greater emphasis upon a global perspective in their students through education, including graduate-level education (e.g., CGS Global Summits, survey data and reports; APLU's global Land Grant perspective). To tell a simplified version of the story, international programs at U.S. colleges and universities began initially with Study Abroad experiences and have expanded to involve undergraduate, graduate and professional students, and faculty (academic staff) across the missions of the university (learning, discovery, engagement). The various organizational structures (e.g., centralized office for international partnership or decentralized) of universities can and do influence the manner through which collaborations are built and sustained. The process for identifying and selecting partner institutions varies. The process for approving and renewing collaborations varies. The terminology for collaborations also varies although similarities between concepts do exist.

Graduate international collaborations can be categorized under the following broad headings based upon the purpose and type of the partnership:

- Recruitment, admissions and scholarship,
- Research and scholarly projects,
- International experiences for graduate students and faculty, including short-term employment, and
- Formal degree-focused collaborations.

Each of these should be considered as value-added components to the university's efforts toward internationalization and the complexity varies in relationship to the particular collaboration.

Many U.S. universities have established formal relationship with international agencies or universities for the primary purpose of recruiting and enrolling international students. Examples include written agreements with CONACYT (National Council on Science and Technology) for Mexican students to receive scholarships to pursue graduate degrees in science and technology fields. Another example is the Vietnam Education Foundation (VEF), a U.S. independent federal agency established to "strengthen the U.S.-Vietnam bilateral relationship through educational exchanges in science and technology."[1] Similarly, universities have entered into formal agreements with entities from foreign countries (e.g., Saudi Arabia) for the sole purpose of securing admission to graduate degrees by the foreign nationals and providing scholarships through degree completion.

Through their academic pursuits and those of their students, faculty often have the occasion to engage with colleagues with similar interests around the world. These networks can lead to collaboration on research projects, grants and publications, and virtual and in-country experiences for graduate students and faculty. These types of experiences might provide the spark for increasing interest in additional international experiences and greater global understanding.

Other types of international experiences for graduate students include a more traditional Study Abroad experience, semester in residence, or summer intensive experience in a foreign country. These sometimes take the forms of formal exchange programs in which students from each partner institution/country send students abroad to study for a limited period of time before returning to their home institution. Exchanges can be focused on education and coursework based experiences as well as research intensive, project based experiences. In addition, graduate degree programs could include a specified and university-organized educational experience such as an international experience required in selected MBA programs or a future professoriate course on global perspectives taught outside of the United States. International travel programs for faculty are also available, opportunities through which faculty can explore research and educational collaborations with partner universities across multiple disciplines. Finally, some partnerships can result in opportunities for graduate students to be employed to teach summer classes in a foreign country (e.g., partnership between Virginia Tech and the American University of Kuwait).

The final category concerns formal collaborative degree programs. Under this heading can be found degree programs (or graduate certificates) that are extensions of existing graduate degrees offered in an international setting at a partner institution (e.g., university, agency), new graduate degrees offered

---

1    Vietnam Education Foundation Website, http://home.vef.gov/about_home.php

only in an international context, and formal transfer of credit from enrollment in a partner university resulting in a graduate degree from the U.S. university. Increasingly more common are joint and dual degrees and their variations. In general, dual degree programs are those in which the students enroll at the partner universities and receive a diploma from each university upon completion of the requirements for the two degrees. Joint degree programs involve enrollment at multiple universities and the issuance of a single diploma representing both (or more) universities. For more detailed information about the results of a recent CGS survey on joint and dual degrees, see the article by Denecke and Kent titled *The Graduate International Collaborations Project: A North American Perspective on Joint and Dual Degree Programs,* published in the October 2009 issue of the *CGS Communicator.*[2]

Although the value of international graduate collaborations for today's society and tomorrow's future is readily acknowledged and the opportunities for collaboration are abundant, many challenges exist in building and sustaining such collaborations. As we move forward with collaborations, the following need to be considered:

- Process and procedures for securing official approvals – MOU, MOA, university, state, regional accreditation and professional accreditation
- University policies and procedures regarding admission requirements, academic plans of study, residency requirements, official examinations, committee membership, transfer credit, official transcripts, diplomas, satisfying degree requirements, one thesis or two, archiving of scholarly work (e.g., thesis/dissertation, ETD), etc.
- Faculty credentials for teaching and advising students; faculty visits to partner institutions
- Financial resources – tuition, stipend and assistantships, financial exchange, faculty compensation
- Academic year/summer (e.g., August – May, October – July)
- Graduate Honor system and student life policies
- Administrative support and necessary resources (human, financial); faculty support and participation in programs; workload and acknowledgement of effort; access to university resources
- Assessment and evaluation of collaborative programs

---

2   See CGS Website, www.cgsnet.org/portals/0/pdf/comm_2009_10.pdf, or the full report, *Joint Degrees, Dual Degrees, and International Research Collaborations: A Report on the CGS International Collaborations Project* (CGS: 2010).

- Language competence or not; language of instruction; cultural competence and understanding; differing terminology
- Length of time needed for degree completion
- Research protocols including data collection and storage, human subjects review, animal use and care in research, mentoring, etc.
- Intellectual property issues, copyright, ethical and professional standards, Responsible Conduct of Research (RCR) guidelines; authorship credit and acknowledgement
- Health insurance, housing, stipend, tuition, program fees, living expenses/logistics; visa issues and restrictions if any; dependents and family issues
- Mutual respect and benefit for partners, clear and frequent communication, on-site visits, reviews and evaluation
- Clearly articulated roles and responsibilities of partners; central office with support of senior administration

With these challenges come opportunities to propose and implement innovation solutions to international collaborations. Ours is a global society and graduate education can play a significant role in advancing knowledge and understanding and solving the complex problems facing today's society.

# III. BEGINNING THE PROCESS: HOW DO INSTITUTIONS ENSURE QUALITY, COMPARABILITY, AND SUSTAINABILITY PRIOR TO START-UP?

## Summary of Presentations and Group Discussion

For most universities, the first steps in the process of creating a graduate international collaboration can be the most critical. The start-up phase requires universities to seek more information about their potential partners and to engage in serious reflection about their own institutional goals and needs. The second panel of the Global Summit addressed some of the major topics and questions that universities face when initiating a new collaboration or conducting strategic planning for international initiatives:

- *Assessing Needs and Benefits*: How can graduate international collaborations benefit your institution?
- *Coordinating Efforts at Home*: What role do university leaders play in creating graduate international collaborations at your institution?
- *Partner Selection and Matching*: How does your university select or approve potential partners?
- *Communicating with a Potential Partner*: How are the roles of each partner defined prior to implementation? What structures are put into place?

The panel presentations built upon one of the central conclusions of the first panel—the need to understand the "why" behind collaboration—but they also examined the specific ways that universities could benefit from graduate international collaborations. Presentations by **Barbara Evans** (University of British Columbia) and **William Russel** (Princeton University) outlined benefits such as enhancement of institutional research profiles, expansion of resources, and engagement with some of the most pressing international research questions, and considered some requirements for these partnerships to be successful. **Dr. Russel** also provided a case history from Princeton that detailed the expected and unexpected benefits of the university's strategic international initiatives.

Addressing the next three topics, panelists discussed the specific organizational practices that may help institutions maximize benefits for institutions, faculty, and students. **Jeffery Gibeling** (University of California, Davis) and **Philip Langlais** (Old Dominion University) discussed the strategies they have used at their universities to coordinate the administration of collaborative programs. **Dr. Gibeling** emphasized that graduate deans must work to create a larger group of stakeholders that remain in close communication about operational details, while **Dr. Langlais** focused on the importance of the MOU process as the foundation and reference point for each collaborative activity and record of expected measurable outcomes. Next, **Dorris Robinson-Gardner** (Jackson State University) and **John Keller** (University of Iowa) spoke to the ways in which their universities have selected potential partners in relation to the larger missions of their institutions, and **Mary Ritter** (Imperial College London) described her university's efforts to define partner roles prior to program implementation.

In the discussion, many comments reflected the view that it is easier to assess the value and benefits of a particular collaborative activity when one places that activity in the context of a broader set of institutional activities and priorities. University leaders must pay close attention to the specific goals and benefits of a particular collaboration, but should not become so focused on programmatic details that they lose sight of the broader institutional goals that a program may meet currently and in the future.

Participants reflected on a number of ways to achieve this balance between a focus on specific programs and a focus on larger institutional goals. The first approach was to assess the potential benefits of a collaborative activity in relation to larger set of institutional goals for internationalization. Both **Maxwell King** (Monash University) and **Karen DePauw** (Virginia Tech) said that institutional and strategic plans have helped their universities assess the value of particular collaborations before programs have been implemented.

The second approach was to compare a proposed collaboration to programs that already exist—both domestic and international—when deciding whether it brings added value to the university. **Andrew Comrie** (University of Arizona) noted that such comparisons make it easier for graduate leaders to recognize the unique benefits and limitations of a particular collaborative activity. Different international activities have different life cycles, he observed, and together make up an evolving "ecosystem." This metaphor suggests that not all collaborations are meant to last, and that some informal collaborations may live longer than expected.

Finally, several delegates observed that each collaboration should be considered in relation to both current and *potential* international activities, since the benefits of one collaboration often extend beyond the life of a formal program. **Allison Sekuler** (McMaster University) commented that current collaborative activities may produce unexpected benefits down the road, as when international graduate students become part of larger international networks after returning to their home countries. On the whole, these comments reflected a tendency towards "systems thinking," which can help university leaders accept setbacks at the level of individual programs and remain ready to embrace new opportunities.

The next major discussion strand concerned the strategies for internal coordination of collaborative activities first presented by **Dr. Langlais** and **Dr. Keller**. Participants noted that at some universities, the graduate dean's office may be the nexus of all communications regarding graduate-level collaborations, while at others, this responsibility is shared by a steering committee composed of senior administrators with oversight for international strategy. **Patrick Osmer** (Ohio State University) observed that distributing responsibility for collaboration among university leaders can provide momentum and efficiency to each initiative, especially when key individuals meet on a regular basis. Several participants also pointed out that it is particularly important to ensure close coordination between those responsible for graduate academic affairs and those responsible for research. As in the first session, it was noted that strong administrative coordination is compatible with a "bottom-up" approach to collaboration as long as university leaders provide clear but flexible parameters for faculty-initiated partnerships.

The last major topic of discussion addressed the need to ensure that opportunities for international experience exist for all groups of graduate students. **Thomas Jørgensen** (European University Association) and **Douglas Peers** (York University) pointed out that many graduate students are not able to travel due to family obligations and financial constraints, and that universities must think of ways to make international experience more widely accessible. **Debra Stewart** (CGS) added that there are many opportunities for universities to take advantage of the international diversity that already exists within their institutions, and invited participants to share methods for reaching students with limited mobility. **Dr. DePauw** said that new technologies can play a crucial role in helping students and faculty form global relationships without traveling, and they can also provide wider access to global resources.

Panel two concluded with a number of remarks about the need for internationally-comparable principles for designing programs. As **Kyung-Chan Min** (Yonsei University) observed, "From now on we need to think about how to develop together, not just by our own strategies, so that in the long-run we have more collective benefits for our future." Participants returned to this need for comparability in the fourth and fifth panel sessions, which addressed specific strategies for creating networks between international universities and other stakeholders.

# Assessing Benefits And Needs
## of Graduate International Collaborations

**Barbara Evans**
**University of British Columbia**

There are many kinds of international experience that are of value to graduate students, including collaborative research in a different institution, research fieldwork, gaining access to specific equipment or resources (such as databases and libraries), participating in taught courses including professional training programs, and enrolling in shared academic programs (joint and double degrees). At a less formal level, international conferences provide an opportunity for networking and communication with international colleagues in a particular field of research.

International institutional collaboration relating to graduate students and their academic programs has increased greatly over recent years. The stakeholders in these collaborations are the graduate students themselves, faculty, institutions, communities, nations, and the global research enterprise, but their development rests largely at the institutional level. The underlying purposes of establishing and participating in these collaborations may be quite different for the different stakeholders. Thus, from an institutional perspective, developing effective graduate international collaborations requires the consideration of many factors at a variety of levels.

## Benefits

Why would an institution choose to develop international collaborations at the graduate level? What value might it add and who benefits? How could the success of such programs be measured?

From the perspective of the *university*, graduate international collaboration provides a mechanism to

- support the international goals of the University
- raise the University's research profile and visibility internationally
- enhance the University's research effort (graduate students are after all 'the research engines' of universities)
- support ongoing research collaborations and the development of

new collaborations
- provide access for top research students to unique and/or sophisticated research equipment and resources, and to world-class faculty
- allow students to undertake research of explicit global significance
- facilitate international academic study and experience
- enhance the recruitment of excellent graduate students
- produce more informed global citizens and the next generation of scholars, researchers and leaders

For *students*, a successful international experience can be simply life-changing, developing a student's personal attributes of international leadership, partnership and global engagement. Returning students regularly report increases in confidence in their own academic work, knowledge of the cutting edges of their discipline, breadth of experience, networking skills and connections. The returning graduate's international experience can also extend beyond his or her own research group. They exemplify these enhanced qualities to the benefit of undergraduate students through their frequent roles in tutoring and mentoring, and with other graduate students outside their own group, for example in interdisciplinary activities and professional development programs.

Benefits for the *global community* arise from the work of universities. Many universities in more established education systems deliberately aim to contribute to 'global good' – to the development of a global civil society – by working more constructively with partners in developing countries than in the past.

Also a general goal of graduate education today must surely be to educate students to be contributing members of *society* 10-15 or more years hence. Thus, as we develop graduate international collaborative programs, we must focus on anticipating the future work environment and preparing our students to be effective in that environment.

## The Needs

Effective international collaboration requires knowing our own purposes, perspectives, goals and constraints; understanding those of potential partner universities; and having the strategies, resources and will to make it work. Graduate collaborations thus need to be strongly embedded in the overall international policy of each university – including how the institution wishes to interact internationally. For graduate international collaboration to be successful, it is important that institutions explicitly recognize and reward these activities of faculty through internal promotion policies and practices.

Countries differ greatly in educational policy oversight and in their level of independence at national, regional and institutional levels. Developing countries understandably have different national and institutional goals – their educational, economic and national histories have evolved differently. The relative importance of national interest, institutional development and individual benefit thus varies greatly. These factors lead to differences that impact directly on opportunities for productive international graduate collaboration. When considering establishing international collaborations, it is essential that both partners understand and are sensitive to these differences. The challenge for institutions is to collaborate internationally in a globally ethical manner, while also continuing to serve their own nation's interests.

Graduate education is often also driven (and at least partially funded) by regional and national governments and their goals. Most effective are those situations where regular communication and a practice of consultation exist between governments and universities.

There are considerable global differences in graduate and particularly doctoral education that will potentially impact on international collaborative arrangements including

- the academic structure and requirements of programs, which are linked to local secondary and undergraduate education systems,
- the extent and sources of funding of students and programs,
- government recognition and funding of 'research training,'
- the expected length of the program,
- the nature of the examination,
- the use of external examiners,
- expectations and opportunities related to TA and RA work, and
- demand for training in 'generic skills.'

For procedural consistency and efficiency, the development of internationally endorsed broad 'principles' or 'guidelines' to underpin international graduate collaborations, including expectations for handling visiting students, would be particularly valuable. They would enable the development of opportunities for collaboration within an understood framework and would mean that institutions would not need to start 'from scratch' every time. Such guidelines could also provide indicators of educational requirements and credit arrangements, and thus a measure of transparency and equity for students and programs.

Adequate funding is needed to provide quality international experiences for students and many universities have funds set aside for this purpose. Additional funding is also often available from research agencies and governments. It is reasonable, responsible and important for quality assurance to require a student to provide a written report on the outcomes of the experience upon their return.

Most universities have well-developed marketing and recruitment strategies for international students, but strategies for providing support for these students after they arrive are frequently less well developed. Planning for new collaborative programs should always incorporate ways to measure the quality of outcomes, sustainability and success, and these evaluations should lead directly to refinement and improvement.

# Assessing Needs and Benefits at Princeton and Beyond

## William B. Russel
## Princeton University

Excerpted from **Princeton in the World**, Shirley M. Tilghman & Christopher L. Eisgruber October 17, 2007[1]

Everyone is talking about globalization, and it is easy to understand why. People, products, information, capital, cultural artifacts, social trends, pollutants, and pathogens are all circulating throughout the world with dizzying speed. Domains from business to the arts, from politics to medicine, are becoming more intensely and self-consciously international than ever before. Local knowledge and regional differences remain important, of course. Yet, it is almost impossible to imagine how any contemporary community or ecosystem could be like the Galapagos Islands of Darwin's day, wholly buffered against influences from the outside world. Today local traits and customs mix with and define themselves in relation to global forces and patterns of activity.

To flourish in this environment, Princeton — and, indeed, America's universities and colleges more generally — will have to find ways to meet the challenges of internationalization. Students will have to be knowledgeable about, and comfortable interacting with, cultures different from their own. Researchers will have to become more attentive to international issues and more sensitive to the international dimensions of domestic problems. Faculty will have to recognize that their potential collaborators and rivals will come from not only familiar institutions in the United States and Europe, but also a host of new, and newly vigorous, universities throughout the world. [...]

The accelerating speed of change in the world means that we must continually assess and enhance our effectiveness in the ways we engage the world. In 2003, after reviewing reports from an internal faculty committee and an outside review committee, we concluded that an integrated approach to international and regional studies was needed, so that faculty taking global approaches to issues such as trade and global governance could benefit from the thinking of others who focus on specific regions of the world, and *vice versa*. The Princeton Institute for International and Regional Studies (PIIRS) grew out of these deliberations, with its mission to conduct collaborative, interdisciplinary research and teaching projects that help to integrate

---

1   For the full report, see  Princeton University Reports, Princeton University Website,
    http://www.princeton.edu/reports/globalization-20071017/

international relations and regional studies approaches. With the benefit of energetic leadership from its founding director, Professor Miguel Centeno, and his successor, Professor Katherine Newman, PIIRS is catalyzing new and exciting work in these fields.

If Princeton is to participate fully in the challenges and opportunities that await us in the years ahead, more changes are needed. Every department in the University, not just those specifically concerned with international topics, has the potential to embrace a more international outlook. For that reason, in 2006-07 we requested two additional reports about how Princeton could improve its response to globalization. We convened a special faculty committee to prepare a confidential report on the broad topic of how to "develop a set of strategic priorities and specific measures that will enable the University to fully realize [its] aspiration to be an American university with a broad international vision." Jeremy Adelman, the Chair of Princeton's Department of History, and Anne-Marie Slaughter, the Dean of the Woodrow Wilson School of Public and International Affairs, agreed to chair the Committee, which included faculty members from every division of the University. [...]

The Adelman-Slaughter Committee and the Dean of the College have proposed that Princeton embark on concerted efforts to enhance its international dimensions in ways that preserve and extend the University's traditional strengths. The Adelman-Slaughter Committee articulated a distinctive model of an international scholarly enterprise. The Committee's members envisioned a rich exchange of scholars, students, and ideas across international borders along fluid pathways defined by the research and educational interests of our community, not by inflexible investments in overseas campuses or specific regions of the world. [...] These recommendations chart a course that Princeton must pursue if it aspires to sustain or enhance its standing in the world and provide excellence in teaching and research that will make a real difference in the decades ahead. [...]

## Princeton's Distinctive Mission

[...] In the words of the Committee, "Princeton is an outstanding research university with a deep commitment to superb teaching. It is distinctive in the breadth of its research excellence, the intensity of its engagement with students at all levels, and the close-knit character of its community." Princeton's response to globalization must build upon these attributes. We cannot simply borrow strategies that have been deployed by other American institutions, because we are different in several important ways from our peers. Princeton focuses more on fundamental research and on its undergraduate and doctoral programs, without large professional schools in law, business, and medicine that have played a leading role in international ventures at other American universities. Likewise, Princeton is smaller than many of its peers. Our size facilitates cross-disciplinary collaboration, but it also requires us to choose carefully when we decide what kinds of overseas programs we most want [...] Perhaps most importantly, Princeton's ethos nurtures and depends upon a rich and demanding form of community. We insist that our faculty be present on the campus and in the classroom, and our students often develop such strong loyalties to the institution that they are reluctant to spend time away from it.

Because of these characteristics, the most successful ventures at Princeton have always been "bottom-up" rather than "top-down." They have emerged out of the scholarly expertise, interests, and passions of our faculty and the educational needs of their students rather than from a centrally designed administrative plan. Not surprisingly, the reports from the Adelman-Slaughter Committee [...] emphasized the need to stimulate and facilitate faculty-driven proposals to internationalize Princeton's research and teaching agenda. Such efforts will require more work and creativity than a one-size-fits-all university initiative, but that investment will be well justified: the resulting initiatives will be more likely to flourish in Princeton's unique academic culture.

## "Networks and Flows"

The Adelman-Slaughter Committee offered a compelling vision for how Princeton can build on its strengths and core values to meet the challenges of globalization. Their recommendations were organized around three basic principles:

- *"Internationalization should be nimble and flexible, avoiding heavy sunk costs in institutions."* The Committee emphasized that Princeton's tradition is "to facilitate, not regulate." It counseled the University to avoid investments in satellite campuses that might ultimately do more to constrain than to enable valuable scholarly efforts. As the Committee wrote, "in the long run, we will be distinguished more by the research we promote than by our management of institutions that too often outlive their original inspirations."
- *"The framework for internationalization should enable and support faculty-driven activity."* In the international domain, as elsewhere,

Princeton must permit research and teaching priorities to shape the ventures it launches. The Committee rightly observed that "research and exchanges work best at Princeton when the stakeholders are also the initiators and custodians of their efforts." It accordingly urged the University to "mobilize latent scholarly resources by encouraging faculty and students to reach out and realize ambitions that would otherwise remain in their filing cabinets or e-mail directories."

- *"Internationalization requires an infusion of leadership, resources, and commitment."* The Committee called upon the University to raise substantial new funds to support international initiatives. It also highlighted the need for effective governance mechanisms and administrative leadership to ensure that these resources are well deployed and that the University presses forward the "major transformation" of policies needed to realize its international aspirations.

As the Committee noted, these three principles "share a common theme: the importance of investing in Princeton's *general* capacity for international exchanges and research, rather than concentrating on any particular region, country, or field of research." The Committee called upon the University to encourage "networks and flows" of faculty and students world-wide, lowering the barriers that inhibit our students and faculty from going abroad, and for scholars from other countries coming to Princeton. By bringing visitors from abroad, the University will nurture relationships between its own faculty members and students and their foreign counterparts. These relationships will lead naturally to research collaborations, and they will enrich the content and impact of the experiences that Princeton undergraduates and graduate students will enjoy when they go abroad. By increasing the "porosity" of the campus through increases in both export and import of people and ideas, we will ensure that Princeton's scholarly energy will be felt throughout the world.

## Stimulating New International Projects and Partnerships

The Adelman-Slaughter Committee emphasized that if Princeton wishes to generate innovative research and educational projects that address the challenges of globalization, it must make substantial new investments to support such activity. Princeton must take steps to encourage faculty members to think about opportunities to steer their research and teaching in international directions. And it must ensure that when faculty members and graduate students design research projects with an international dimension, they can find institutional support for their efforts. The Committee highlighted several different kinds of resources that it regarded as crucial to the achievement of these goals.

*Bringing International Visitors to the Princeton Faculty.* The Committee urged Princeton to create a new set of faculty positions that would bring to campus a distinguished cadre of international scholars who would visit on a recurring basis. These "Global Scholars" would come to Princeton for visits of varying duration: some professors, for example, might come for one semester in each of three consecutive years; other professors might come for a shorter span — say, half a semester — in multiple years. While at Princeton, these professors would be expected to teach or co-teach courses; participate in ongoing workshops; and give at least one public presentation, in a workshop or lecture, each time they visited.

The Committee imagined that "the Global Scholars would bring vital new voices from abroad to our departments and classrooms. In addition, the program would inaugurate and sustain durable ties between Princeton and academic centers of excellence around the world. One faculty member in the Humanities described these benefits of exchanges to the Committee: 'More doors would ultimately be opened for us abroad, and our own campus would look and feel and sound a little different, if we made greater room for bringing the best foreign scholars to Princeton.'"

The benefits of the Global Scholars program will be many and lasting. For example, when they return to their home countries, the Global Scholars will help to raise Princeton's profile there. Their visits to Princeton, moreover, will catalyze collaborations that will bring Princeton faculty members, graduate students, and undergraduates overseas. In effect, we will be establishing a vigorous form of academic free trade, in which a robust import policy will go hand-in-hand with a robust export strategy, and ideas will flow freely across international borders. The Committee emphasized that if the international visitors are to play this catalytic role effectively, they must be fully integrated into campus life. For that reason, the Committee insisted that the visitors should return to Princeton for multiple years so that they have a chance to attract a following among students and to build relationships with faculty members. [...]

**Facilitating International Flows of Graduate Students.** The Committee highlighted the critical role of graduate education in any plan for internationalizing Princeton. The Committee recognized that Princeton's graduate student body is already remarkably internationally diverse. Princeton should seize opportunities to capitalize on this diversity. The Committee also expressed an expectation that "much of the movement through our research networks will be conducted by younger scholars, post-doctoral fellows, and — especially — graduate students." The Committee counseled Princeton to provide resources to support international research projects of Princeton graduate students and to facilitate visits by foreign graduate students who might come to Princeton to collaborate on research or educational projects. These resources would include travel grants and fellowships for Princeton students who need to extend their term of study to do research abroad; funds to defray the costs of having visiting foreign graduate students; and short-term housing. […]

## Conclusion

Globalization presents universities with great opportunities and challenges. It generates a fascinating new array of problems for researchers to analyze and students to study. It calls upon universities to rethink their missions and practices so that they can supply the leadership and analysis needed to solve problems with an international dimension. It demands that universities prepare their students to become worldly cosmopolitans. And it promises to generate strong universities around the world who can be partners and who will also be rivals to their American peers.

Yet, globalization also presents risks for universities. […] If Princeton is to flourish in the 21st century, it must meet the challenges of globalization in a way that is both vigorous and consistent with traditions and practices that define our scholarly community. The Adelman-Slaughter Committee has mapped an approach to globalization well-adapted to Princeton's distinctive commitment to an intense scholarly community of teaching and research. The Committee's ideas constitute a coherent and powerful approach that will, in its own words, transform Princeton into "a center for a multitude of scholarly networks humming with activity and effectively responding to changes in scholarship and the vagaries of world affairs, while creatively defining the cutting edges of global research." That is the right international vision for Princeton, and we should pursue it.

# Coordinating Efforts at Home: Reflections from the University of California, Davis

## Jeffery C. Gibeling
## University of California, Davis

While there are some significant examples of long-standing international partnerships in graduate education, the number of such efforts has expanded greatly in recent years. However, there remains much potential for further development of international collaborations. Thus, it is necessary that universities continue to develop the internal structures to coordinate efforts "at home."

In order to capitalize on international opportunities, many universities now have offices of international programs that were established to promote a wide array of international interactions between institutions. However, these international offices are relatively new additions to the administrative structure and may not be directly connected to or integrated with the academic and administrative structures that are traditionally responsible for undergraduate and graduate education on the campus. One key to successfully managing international collaborations is to ensure that the international programs office is led by a senior academic administrator who can represent the university to external contacts, who has credibility with the faculty within the university and who has the vision and leadership skills to develop a sound academic strategy for international collaborations. He or she must also have a strong understanding of current higher education activities in various countries and connections to key government and university officials around the world. Finally, the senior international programs officer must also ensure that the University mission and strategic plans include goals to strengthen international collaborations.

Successful international collaborations may be initiated at the faculty level (from the ground up), between Presidents, Rectors or Chancellors (from the top down) or at intermediate administrative levels within the organizations. Whatever the point of origin, it is important that all stakeholders are aware of the formal and informal interactions between the partner institutions or countries. The risk is that collaborations that start from the ground up will not flourish without institutional support and partnerships that are initiated from the top down will fail to provide the faculty interactions that are critical for success.

Thus, in order to fully develop partnerships with another country, it is essential to understand the full range of relationships between the university and institutions within that country. The University of California, Davis has a rich tradition of international collaborations, derived largely from its founding as an agricultural campus. But, these collaborations now cover a much broader set of disciplines including the humanities, social sciences, engineering, law and medicine. That means that there is a multitude of pre-existing connections to many countries throughout the world. Sometimes, it can be a challenge to identify them. One key strategy to facilitate understanding of the multiple international relationships is to ensure that the Office of International Programs maintains an international faculty database. Using information provided by the individual faculty members, anyone on or off campus can readily identify who at UC Davis has a relationship to any particular country and might be an important partner in developing a relationship with that country.

For international collaborations at the graduate level, the Graduate Dean plays a critical role of translating the interests of the on- and off-campus partners into operational programs. The Graduate Dean and staff in the graduate office understand the policies and practices that can aid or interfere with successful collaborations. The Graduate Dean is also the conduit to gaining Academic Senate and administrative approval for new academic graduate programs. At UC Davis, the role of the Graduate Dean in international partnerships represents an expansion of activities related to traditional on-campus programs. As is the case at many other institutions, the question of who pays for students' exchanges is central to the successful implementation of an agreement. The Graduate Dean is the person most naturally poised to understand the broad academic and financial implications of this question and to translate the desires of faculty to develop a formal academic collaboration with another institution into agreements that have the support of other administrative offices that have a role to play in their implementation.

However, the Graduate Dean cannot act alone or even serve as a clearinghouse for information. It is essential to assemble a group of interested participants to help plan and guide any potential international collaboration. As an example, UC Davis has established a Chile-UC Davis Partnerships Steering Committee to guide interactions between our university and universities in Chile as well as the BECAS CHILE program that awards fellowships to promising students from Chile who wish to pursue graduate education at partner universities, including UC Davis. While this is not directly an academic collaboration, the strategy is sufficiently flexible to serve as a model for a variety of types of international collaborations. The Chile-UC Davis

Partnerships Steering Committee is chaired by the Vice Provost for International Programs and includes among its membership the Dean of Graduate Studies, the Associate Dean for International Programs from the College of Agricultural and Environmental Sciences, several faculty members with continuing research interests in Chile (including the Director of the Hemispheric Institute on the Americas) and an Executive Director. UC Davis is fortunate to have a former graduate student and Chilean citizen to serve as the Executive Director to help guide the partnership and coordinate the activities of the Steering Committee. The group meets once per quarter, with frequent email updates, and also helps to host visitors from the Chilean government, universities and the BECAS CHILE program. It is important to recognize that the Steering Committee serves to coordinate academic initiatives with institutions in Chile, but is not a replacement for nor does it have any of the authorities granted to standing committees that govern academic matters. The key functions served by this Steering Committee are to remain aware of the multiple research activities of faculty in Chile, facilitate connections to Chilean universities, publicize the fellowship program, promote UC Davis within targeted partner universities in Chile and coordinate resolution of administrative issues within UC Davis and with the Chile partners.

Although different universities may find other structures to be useful, the examples cited here currently serve the needs of international collaborations at UC Davis. Of course, this is a very dynamic area within our institution, as at many others, and the ways of coordinating "at home" will certainly evolve in the near future.

# Coordinating Efforts at Home: Strategies at Old Dominion University

### Philip J. Langlais
### Old Dominion University

At Old Dominion University, the creation and implementation of graduate international collaborations are coordinated through the establishment of an International Memorandum of Understanding (IMOU). The Vice Provost for Graduate Studies and Research coordinates the terms of the IMOU, obtains approval by all appropriate institutional units at ODU and insures agreement from the appropriate officials of the international university, academy or institute. Careful attention is paid to obtaining approval by faculty, college deans, university counsel, registrar, international services, SACS liaison, VP for Research, VP for Budget and Finance, the Provost and President of the University. Depending on the type of IMOU and the level of complexity, arriving at a signed IMOU may take as little as a few months to as long as two years from the initial expression of mutual interest.

We have basically two levels of IMOUs at ODU. The first is an agreement to pursue the establishment of an academic and/or research partnership for the purpose of carrying out various collaborative programs. The second level of IMOU describes the terms and details of a commitment to deliver specific academic and/or research programs and collaborations.

Our IMOU with the Indian Institute of Technology Kanpur (IITK) (India) is an example of the first type of agreement and identifies the following four "Priority Areas of Cooperation:

- Establishing a faculty exchange program to facilitate the sharing of teaching and research agendas among colleagues at both institutions;
- Establishing a student exchange, both long-term and short-term, at both the undergraduate and graduate level, based on reciprocity and mutual interest;
- Co-sponsoring workshops, symposia and conferences; and,
- Facilitating joint publication of scholarly articles on topics of mutual interest. This IMOU makes no commitment of resources or deliverables. Rather it establishes a platform for pursuing the development of collaborations in specific areas of mutual interest. Within the framework of this IMOU, faculty and administrators are

given the approval and a set of guidelines by which to pursue more specific agreements. In this IMOU both ODU and IITK have agreed that more detailed IMOUs need to be negotiated before specific joint activities can begin. Standards terms are included regarding duration, revision, renewal and termination of the IMOU.

The second level of IMOU defines the details of specific programmatic and/or research agreements between ODU and an international university, academy or institute. Our IMOU with the Turkish Air Force Academy (TAFA), Istanbul, Turkey is an example of a cooperative academic degree program. This agreement defines the terms of a Master of Science degree in selected engineering disciplines conferred by ODU's college of engineering on participating students from the Aerospace and Space Technologies Institute (ASTIN) of the TAFA.

The students pursue the cooperative program in three phases that are described in the IMOU. Prior to formal approval and implementation, ODU engineering faculty and my office reviewed and approved a list of ASTIN graduate courses that met our degree learning outcomes and could be used to fulfill the 12 ASTIN transfer credits required to complete phase one. The second phase of training occurs at ODU. To enter into the second phase, students must successfully apply and be admitted to the university and complete the remainder of the courses required by the degree curriculum. Working with our SACS liaison, the VP for budget and finance, the Registrar, Office of International Programs, and Student Affairs, we established a special tuition rate and in turn obtained from ASTIN an agreement to pay the full tuition, housing, health insurance and program administration costs for each student. In this IMOU and others like it, ODU requires that all faculty and students in this program be trained in federal, state and local regulations regarding responsible conduct of research, intellectual property, and export control materials.

Considerable effort and commitment on the part of faculty, along with infrastructure and finances, are required to create an IMOU. Despite the best intentions of all parties involved, implementation of the IMOU can be delayed or worse, the IMOU produces no measurable outcomes. To mitigate these shortcomings, ODU emphasizes to the faculty, department chairs and college deans the expectation that an IMOU will result in measureable outcomes, e.g., enrollments, degrees conferred, published research collaborations. Furthermore, the responsible faculty and administrator are required to provide a semi-annual report on progress made in achieving the goals and outcomes described in the IMOU.

# Selecting and Approving Potential Partners: Jackson State University's Approach

### Dorris R. Robinson-Gardner
### Jackson State University

U.S. universities have been forming global collaborations with international institutions of higher learning for many years. The Fulbright-Hayes Study Abroad program for international exchanges for scholars, graduate students and professionals is one in which many domestic institutions have actively participated since the 1950's. Today, more domestic institutions are forming linkages with international universities thereby creating global opportunities for enhancing student learning and achievement. These linkages often stem from a myriad of connections and often mirror faculty-driven agendas.

Jackson State University's (JSU) history, began within the context of Mississippi's history of racial segregation, a system of exclusion that permeated every aspect of society, including higher education. Nevertheless, the university has made great strides in creating inclusionary initiatives for forming international collaborations and linkages in its 132 year history.

A historically black, Carnegie, doctoral research-intensive public institution, JSU educates a diverse student population drawn from Mississippi, other U.S. states, and many foreign countries. The university consists of a very diverse faculty consisting of academic scholars from Eastern Europe, Africa, Central America, the Caribbean, Latin America, Korea, China, India and Asia. The university offers a broad range of undergraduate and graduate programs in its six (6) colleges. These colleges are: Business; Education and Human Development; Liberal Arts; Lifelong Learning; Public Service; and Science, Engineering and Technology. JSU is a learning community for highly capable students, as well as those who are capable but under-prepared.

Yet, despite our university's overall success JSU still face many challenges in ensuring that our students are appropriately engaged in global education and engaged participants in international collaborations and linkages.

JSU became an aggressive participant in globalization in 1989, even though the university did not have adequate start-up resources to fund the development of global collaborations and linkages. A daring, bold and creative faculty member from the political science department was authorized to develop an Office of International Programs and later created a consortium with three other institutions of higher education. Many institutional faculty members became very aggressive, engaged other international faculty members and sought funding for creating international programs on individual campuses. In 2004, the creation of Exchanges and Linkages Programs was followed by additional Study Abroad initiatives, which enabled the university to form additional global collaborations and linkages.

Ten years later, JSU and the other three institutions of higher education have strong international programs and global collaborations and linkages for the purpose of strengthening faculty resources, internationalizing domestic programs and curricula, providing cutting-edge research experiences for domestic undergraduate and graduate students, securing international faculty and postdoctoral students and broadening participation in the HBCU graduate experience.

The remaining portion of this paper will focus on how an urban, southern university selected and approved global partners, maximized the advantages of global partnerships for increasing the university's visibility, and improved student learning and achievement through the development of global collaborations and linkages.

As collaborations and linkages were formed, numerous questions surfaced regarding building successful models and sustaining them. Many, many questions focused on the issue of sustainability.

How will we choose partners? How does an institution of higher education select an appropriate partner for forming a successful collaboration? What is an appropriate partner in higher education? Who is an appropriate partner? How does one know that they are an appropriate partner for another institution? Is the process mission-oriented and strategically driven?

Where do we begin? Who initiates the process? Why would one want to initiate such a process? What would be the value-added for the university and its faculty? What would be the value-added for the students and staff? Is the process faculty-driven or administration-driven?

Will we be successful? Why would Nobel prize physicists and computational chemists be willing to mentor and co-supervise research activities for domestic doctoral students studying in a developing program? Is it possible to hold international conferences and present research and publish jointly in scientific journals?

What are our assets? How is it that an HBCU located in the SREB region could develop a consortium with three other institutions to attract national resources for the purposes of strengthening faculty resources, internationalizing academic programs and curriculums, and exposing students to a global community? All of these ideas are possible with a committed domestic and international faculty, support from administration, genuine desire to broaden participation in graduate education and adequately prepare graduates for the workforce in a global world.

The global partnerships are very successful and thriving through participation from universities in Eastern Europe, Africa, Central America, Latin America, the Caribbean, Newly Independent States (NIS), China, India and Asia.

Other entities include Nigerian State Governments; the Government of South Africa; British Petroleum; African American Institute; Aurora Associates; the Institute for International Education; National Association of Partners of the Americas; Partners for International Education and Training; Fulbright; the U.S. Department of State; and the Bureau of Educational and Cultural Affairs.

Further, the university and consortium have established global relationships with professional organizations such as the Institute of Economic Affairs (Ghana), the International Institute for Human Rights and Democracy in Africa (Zambian Chapter), the Municipalities of Lugoj and Timisoara in Romania, the City of Rezeknes in Latvia, the Amur Region in Russia, the Dnipropetrovsk Region in Ukraine and the City of Volzhsky in Volgograd Region, Russia.

The university and Consortium have been awarded numerous international human resource development training and technical assistance contracts funded by the U.S. Agency for International Development (USAID), the U.S. Department of State, and the U.S. Department of Education.

Graduate faculty members are engaged in the implementation of international development, training and technical assistance projects in the following areas: Agribusiness Development and Farm Management; Cooperatives and Associations Management; Natural Resource Management; Community and Economic Development; Local Government Administration and Management; Privatization and Economic Restructuring; Small Business Development and Administration; Democratization and Leadership Development; Legislative, Judicial and Legal Reform; Journalism and Media Management in a Democratic Society; Women and Leadership; Civic Education and Citizenship; Development and Management of Non-

Governmental Organizations (NGOs); Higher Education Administration; and English Language Training for Teachers of English and many more. All of these activities engage our undergraduate and graduate students with global opportunities through international partnerships.

Establishing global partnerships is paramount for colleges and universities to provide adequate learning experiences for both undergraduate and graduate students. These experiences typically allow students to become immersed in other languages, cultures and norms and gain a better understanding of their own cultural values and biases. It may also help students to mature by allowing them to gain a stronger sense of independence, confidence and direction and establish lifelong friendships.

# International Academic Partners at the University of Iowa: Partner Selection and Matching

### John C. Keller
### The University of Iowa

At the graduate education level, the University of Iowa has over twenty-five "relationships" with international academic partners. An additional unknown number of relationships exist at the undergraduate and professional degree program levels. None of our current partnerships were the result of an administrative mandate to create such relationships, but rather were started as "grass-root" efforts generated by entrepreneurial faculty. Most of the graduate level relationships are several decades old, and were established after a collaborative faculty relationship with an international colleague was developed and nurtured. At the University of Iowa, the international partner relationships follow several general patterns. First, with several longstanding partnerships, there is a formal exchange where students from their home countries participate in academic exchange programs with peers at a host international institution. Thus, under this arrangement, students of each program benefit from the relationship. Approximately six such programs exist at Iowa, most often with sister institutions in Europe and the Mid-East. Perhaps the most well known of these programs is with the University of Dortmund in Germany, with whom Iowa participates in the Deutscher Akademischer Austausch Dienst (DAAD, German Academic Exchange Service). Students from both institutions have benefited from this mutual exchange in recent years.

Second and more recently, international partnerships with other countries are expanding, as foreign institutions are anxious to establish relationships with high quality and reputable institutions of higher education in the US. Again these relationships start with the nurturing of faculty relationships, based on mutual research and scholarly interests and efforts. The role of the Graduate College in the creation of formalized international partnerships is one dedicated largely to broader issues of "process" rather than to the development of specific programs. The faculty of the individual departments and programs are responsible for the construction and verification of quality for any potential international degree collaboration, in much the same way that they contribute to the creation of new degree programs or make recommendations about the conferral of degrees. The Graduate College, in collaboration with other administrative offices, is responsible for admitting the students, verifying the completion of degree requirements, and setting "boundaries" for the construction of the combined degree program.

At Iowa, these relationships occur at several levels: discipline to discipline, college to college, and university to university. At the graduate level, approximately two dozen relationships exist and in Fall 2009, approximately 20 students were enrolled in collaborative programs. The relationships are often "formalized" with a Memorandum of Understanding that is signed by university officials from both institutions. One popular program has been the "3+2" program, where, after three years at their home school, top undergraduates from the off-shore institution come to Iowa to pursue two years of graduate work. The off-shore institution credits one of the years at Iowa as undergraduate credit leading to that institution's undergraduate degree, while the two years in the graduate program at Iowa leads to the conferral of a master's degree. This 3+2 program has emerged in the past few years in engineering disciplines with several institutions in India and Korea.

The 3+2 program with off-shore institutions follows the emergence of similar program opportunities at Iowa within our engineering departments and other select disciplines on campus. At Iowa, following the long-standing model of master's degree credit counting towards the Ph.D., "combined degree" refers to the fact that at some point in the educational process, academic credit counts towards the conferral of two degrees. For most of our on-campus 3+2 programs, this cross-crediting occurs at the end of the undergraduate curriculum and the beginning of the graduate degree, and a specified number of graduate credits are accepted as elective courses for the undergraduate degree and are also applied to the master's degree. With off-shore institutions, 3+2 programs are slightly different in that no coursework taken before the conferral of the bachelor's degree is ever counted toward the UI master's degree. Thus, off-shore 3+2 agreements are really early admission agreements. The advantages of such partnerships are not only related to the current and future research collaborations created by such efforts, but also to the possibility of recruiting exceptionally well-qualified international students into our doctoral programs. In the long term, international academic partnerships such as these address the University of Iowa's strategic goals to expand its global role of meeting the needs of higher education and fostering an environment of increased collaboration.

The University of Iowa does not, and is not likely to, engage in the creation of "joint" degree programs. Using our terminology, a "joint" degree program is one in which students receive the same two graduate degrees, or a co-signed diploma, from two institutions for the same body of work. On our campus, the foregoing has been viewed as unnecessary, and depending upon the specifics, inappropriate.

# IV. A RANGE OF COLLABORATION STRUCTURES: DIVERSE ADVANTAGES AND CHALLENGES

## Summary of Presentations and Group Discussion

If the first and second summit panels gave attention to the drivers behind graduate international collaborations, the third delved more deeply into the operational questions that arise in different types of collaborative programs. This panel provided an opportunity to examine specific structures of collaboration and their programmatic features, including support services for graduate students and faculty. To help focus the discussion, the panel was divided into two parts, the first on collaboration structures and the second on support services, with discussion periods following each.

## Part I: Collaboration Structures

Different collaborations require varying levels of commitment on the part of universities in terms of time and material resources. Whereas joint and dual degree programs always require long-term planning and a more complex approvals process, research collaborations typically do not involve as many hurdles. Presentations on collaboration structures therefore addressed two different sets of questions corresponding to each structure:

- *"Informal" Research Collaborations and Exchanges*: What issues and challenges are unique to such collaborations? When does it make sense to scale up to a degree-granting program?
- *Joint and Dual Degree Programs*: How are various degree structures defined? What are the relative advantages and challenges of each type in different national contexts?

In addressing informal research collaborations, participants stressed that these partnerships can provide considerable value to universities without the significant commitments that joint and dual degrees require. **Chaohui Du** (Shanghai Jiaotong University) and **Patrick Osmer** (Ohio State University) noted that research collaborations are always built upon strong research relationships between faculty and, because these partnerships are informal, allow universities to become more familiar with one another before making a more significant commitment. As **Dr. Du** phrased it in his presentation, "[…] we cannot overlook the merits of such informal partnerships because they enable us to get to know our cooperative partners and search for the most appropriate direction for collaboration."

Next, presenters examined the philosophies and approaches that guide strategic decision-making about joint and dual degree programs. Although they were addressing three different national and institutional contexts, **Jean Chambaz** (Université Pierre et Marie Curie), **Andrew Comrie** (University of Arizona), and **Douglas Peers** (York University) all concluded that it is important for universities to embark upon these deep collaborations with a certain degree of openness. Dr. Chambaz stated that institutions must build what he termed a culture of "jointness:" the goal should not be to find a partner that organizes programs in the same way as one's home institution, but to promote, on both sides of the collaboration, the flexibility needed to meet shared goals. **Dr. Peers** and **Dr. Comrie** also observed that negotiations between universities should focus less on the means by which program content is delivered (such as credit hours) and more on the outcomes of the collaborative degree. **Dick Strugnell** (University of Melbourne) emphasized that such openness must nevertheless lead to some definitional agreement about degree types and official roles and provided several examples of common definitions used by his university and its partners.

In the discussion that followed presentations on joint and dual degrees, panelists reflected on different approaches to instilling a "joint culture" on one's own campus. **Daniel Denecke** (CGS) noted that while all presenters underlined the need for a flexible attitude toward differences institutional context, their comments also suggested somewhat different ideas about how to adapt to these differences. Some presenters had indicated that it is useful to emphasize similarities between collaborative degree programs and domestic or established degree programs, **Dr. Denecke** observed, while others suggested that joint and dual degrees required institutions to think in radically new ways about the "value-added" of these types of degrees. These differences raised a question: "Are these collaborations really requiring universities to think about innovative structures and to ask fundamental value questions?"

Participants affirmed that this was the case, but added that change may need to be gradual; university leaders may find it helpful to stress what is familiar about a new degree type when working to secure buy-in, or at the outset of the process of building a new degree program. **Dr. Comrie** said that over time, joint and dual degrees have produced significant changes in his own university's culture and in attitudes toward dual-authored dissertations or dissertations that meet requirements in different countries: "We got there through mentally evolutionary steps, even if the results were somewhat revolutionary." **Dr. Chambaz** added that changes in institutional culture can begin with just a few small collaborative programs. The spirit of collaboration can "diffuse" in an institution, he said, and inspire others to pursue similar directions. **Sheila Bonde** (Brown University) also noted that cultural attitudes toward collaborative degree programs often do not begin to shift until a new program has seen some success: "[…] once we have a graduate of [a new] program, I see people relax and say, 'Yes, we recognize the quality of the degree,' and that makes the second step that much easier." Overall, participants indicated that building on successes, and expanding programs incrementally, was a common strategy for managing risk in these deep collaborations.

## Part II: Support Services

In the second half of the panel, participants discussed various approaches to building support services for students and faculty, from services built into collaborative programs to campus-wide resources that may be accessed prior to or during participation. Some graduate institutions build support services for students and faculty into collaborative programs, while others may identify campus-wide resources that students and faculty may use prior to or during their participation in a program. Presenters addressed three topics:

- *Student Support Services*: How are graduate students prepared to pursue study and research abroad? What support services are available?
- *Faculty Support Services*: How are faculty prepared to supervisor or mentor visiting international students?
- *Learning from Undergraduate Programs*: What can we learn from effective international collaborations involving undergraduates?

The presentations addressing these questions recognized that cultural orientation for graduate students and faculty cannot be overlooked in educational and research collaborations. The ability of students and faculty to take full advantage of their experiences abroad and contribute to the success of their programs often depends on what might seem like small practical details. **Dr. Bonde** said that the success of graduate students relies in particular on two areas of preparation: "etiquette" lessons that allow them to assimilate into the new social networks they will encounter, and "ethics" training that sensitizes them to the ethical issues (and impact) of their research.[1] In his presentation on both faculty and student support systems, **Hasuck Kim** (Seoul National University) also stressed the importance of providing written and online resources to visitors, including resources in English. **Susan Stites-Doe** (SUNY Brockport) followed these presentations with a number of ideas for translating undergraduate program features into graduate programs, such as inviting returning students to give presentations about their international experiences to their peers.

The first issue to emerge from the discussion was the appropriate level of support for graduate students participating in international collaborations, particularly those involving travel, study, and research abroad. **Thomas Jørgensen** (European University Association) noted that it is important to give students a "healthy dose of challenge" during their time abroad without replicating the educational experiences they have at home. **Allison Sekuler** (McMaster University) seconded this point and added that universities should keep in mind the value to students of cultural immersion when preparing them for research and study abroad. Foreign language training is an important part of this preparation, **Dr. Sekuler** added, and noted that this element should not be overlooked in exchange programs where English is the dominant professional language, as in the sciences or math. Language training allows a degree of immersion in the culture that students in such programs will not attain if they do not acquire proficiency in the language of the culture in which they are studying and conducting research.

The second topic that received focused attention was the need for universities to find ways to recognize meaningful international experiences that occur outside of formal degree programs. **Debra Stewart** (CGS) asked participants to share their perspectives on formal mechanisms of recognition, and the following methods were cited:

---

1    Dr. Brown noted that the ethics of international research and scholarship, the topic of the 2009 Global Summit, had helped inspire some of the content for an NSF-funded program, "Ethical Awareness in International Collaborations: A Contextual Approach" (NSF# 0933509).

- *Graduate certificates* that validate international research experience or coursework.[2]
- *International internships.* These are typically substantive, formal experiences that may be included on a student's CV.
- *The thesis or dissertation.* If the student's research is international in nature, it formally records the student's international experience in much the same way that credits for coursework in an international program might do.
- *Transcript notation* for courses completed at a partner institution.
- In the UK, a *diploma supplement* called the Higher Education Achievement Record (HEAR). This document has been introduced to record educational experiences beyond traditional credits and degrees, and may include a period of study abroad.

As participants pooled these methods for recognizing international experience, they also discussed the potential value of providing credentials (not just recognition) based on international experience. Some noted that the move toward providing formal credentials should be resisted, and that students should be reminded that transferable skills, such as language proficiency or lab skills, will be valued in and of themselves. At the same time, it was also observed that access to career opportunities may depend for some students on official credentials. **Dr. Jørgensen** said that this is particularly the case in Europe, where there is a high degree of mobility among very different cultures.

In conclusion to the discussion of global professional skills, **Jim McGinty** (Cambridge Information Group) said that a mobility experience is quickly becoming a hiring prerequisite for global firms. He added that universities must develop new ways to equip students seeking jobs outside of academe with both the skills and credentials needed to meet this demand.

The session as a whole indicated that in developing collaborations, the process of reaching consensus about programmatic details often leads universities to test their assumptions about key elements of the graduate experience in their domestic context. Ideally, the process will result in an innovative program that remains consistent with the institutional missions and national priorities of all partners.

---

2    Two participants provided specific examples of such certificates. Karen DePauw (Virginia Tech) described her university's "International Research and Development" certificate, which requires a student to take coursework, spend time studying abroad, and write a thesis with an international component, and John Hayton (Australian Education International) cited the "Global Leadership Certificate" at Macquarie University in Australia, which offers a menu of options through which a student can accumulate the points or credits necessary to earn the credential.

# "Informal" Research Collaborations and Exchanges at Shanghai Jiao Tong University

## Chaohui Du
## Shanghai Jiao Tong University

Informal research collaborations and exchanges now constitute an important part of our graduate study programs. From our practice, we are keenly aware of the unique challenges we must face within them.

China's scientific research and education system tend to lay particular emphasis on the first author sign unit, the first author or the corresponding author, which, to a large extent, discourages researchers from collaborating actively and therefore impedes research collaborations. Meanwhile, for student exchanges, four major problems call our attention. First, the courses selected in the exchange university may not be consistent with the requirements at students' home universities. Owing to the differences between higher education systems, most of the courses completed during the exchange will not be recognized by the home university in China. Second, if tuition fees cannot be covered by scholarship or get waived, it often happens that those academically excellent but financially limited students have to give up the opportunity to enroll in the exchange programs. Third, Chinese universities favor potential partners with complementary strengths. As a result, it is difficult to ensure that both parties send an equal number of students. Fourth, on some occasions, a lack of communication between home and abroad tutors renders exchange students unsupervised.

Despite these problems, we cannot overlook the merits of such informal partnerships because they enable us to get to know our cooperative partners and search for the most appropriate direction for collaboration. As the number of our partners continues to expand, we have been searching for proper ways to manage such individualized exchanges. For example, for the collaboration between tutors, we keep up-to-date with the professors' research progress. As for student exchanges, we keep a record of their exit and entry procedures. In addition, we monitor the evaluation of students' study and consider it an effective way of getting feedback on their progress. If informal collaborations and student exchanges can ensure complementary strengths between our university and our partners while also improving the competitiveness of students, then we think it is time to scale it up to a degree-granting program.

# Informal Research Collaborations and Exchanges at Ohio State University

**Patrick S. Osmer**
**Ohio State University**

## Background

International research collaborations involving one or a small number of faculty members and their graduate students epitomize informal graduate international collaborations. Such "ground-up" collaborations usually grow out of personal contacts based on common research interests and often originate via contacts made during international conferences or through faculty visits to other institutions.

The great strength of these collaborations is that they arise from strong and common interests among the people involved, provide much interaction among the participants, and can be established quickly and flexibly. The participants are strongly motivated. These collaborations can involve good, hands-on experience (field work, laboratory work, library/archival work, etc.) for the participants, which is especially valuable to graduate students. One such example at Ohio State is in astronomy, where graduate students have been involved in broad international collaborations in research and observational work in South Africa, New Zealand, and Tasmania.

These linkages are more research-oriented than they are focused on academic programs. We believe that there are many such strong interactions in the graduate programs. More of them, if they appear to be sustainable over a longer term, could provide the basis for formalized graduate student exchanges and course credit abroad.

Some of these collaborations have already been formalized at Ohio State through "Academic Cooperation Agreements" among the participating institutions. These agreements follow the models already established for undergraduate student exchanges and/or student abroad programs. This process is handled through the Office of International Affairs, which is a resource for the Graduate School as it identifies future proposals for joint or dual degrees. Ohio State's study abroad program in Australia, for example, partners with the University of Melbourne and Charles Sturt University and is targeted toward any Ohio State undergraduate major with an interest in animal production, with the caveat that preference may be given to animal science majors. Parallel research collaborations involving faculty and graduate students also occur, and a proposal to develop these efforts into a joint graduate degree program in animal science is now underway.

For joint degrees at the graduate level, we look for each partner institution to bring complementary expertise to the proposed program. Ohio State's existing graduate student exchange agreements with three universities in Iceland are the sort of arrangement that could develop into a joint degree. The current graduate student agreement with the University of Iceland, Reykjavik, is very specific about the expertise brought by each partner. Written on behalf of the School of Environment and Natural Resources (Ohio State) and on behalf of the Faculty of Life and Environmental Sciences and the Faculty of Earth Sciences (UI), the purpose of this exchange agreement is "to prepare graduate students in theoretical principles and practice skills" and is focused on the unique geological feature of both geographic locations and the research expertise of each faculty group. At UI, graduate students study the "physiographic and environmental characteristics of arctic and sub-arctic biomes in Iceland in relation to climate change and carbon dynamics...." At Ohio State, graduate students study "soil organic matter dynamics in relation to soil quality; off-setting $CO_2$ emissions; measurement and validation of C pool and fluxes under field and laboratory conditions ... in the Ohio River Basin." The genuinely complementary capabilities of both institutions result in a stronger cross-institutional effort and academic experience.

Ohio State has standard procedures for graduate student travel and participation in these efforts on a short-term basis. For instance, international graduate students on these exchanges at Ohio State must enroll on a non-degree basis.

## Issues and challenges

A central issue stemming from this "bottom-up" approach is how to provide and ensure long-term commitment to an existing collaboration when desirable. Doing so requires an institutional commitment beyond the individual faculty to faculty level, which is subject to changes in individual circumstances.

Getting a good inventory of such international research collaborations at Ohio State is a challenge because of the fluid nature of the collaborations. Some are formalized in the way that many undergraduate study abroad and student exchanges are formalized; others are less formal (faculty to faculty) and do not make it onto the radar at the Graduate School or university level.

Issues begin to arise when participants wish to develop and formalize graduate work, e.g., student exchanges, credit for course work in the other institution, and the possibility of dual or joint degrees. Where we have seen problems (from the Graduate School's perspective) is when a graduate program moves ahead on its own and establishes what it believes to be a formal agreement for a collaboration and then finds out that additional vetting by the Graduate School, university, and State of Ohio is likely required.

Ohio State is beginning to develop protocols for dual and joint degrees, which require good definition to maintain academic quality and standards. The success of this project will require the involvement of the faculty, the Graduate School, Office of Academic Affairs, and Office of International Affairs, and the appropriate committee in the Ohio Board of Regents. Effective, on-going communications about this process and the resulting protocols will be essential.

In addition, Ohio State is developing plans to establish "gateways" initially in three areas of the world (India, China, and Brazil) where we already have significant research and educational efforts. Staffed by Ohio State representatives, the "Global Gateways" offices are expected to provide a base for the further development of research and educational collaborations.[1]

---

1    For more information about Ohio State's "Global Gateways" project, please see the website of the Ohio State Office of International Affairs at http://oia.osu.edu/gateways.html

# Dual and Joint PhD Degrees:
# A University of Melbourne Perspective

**Dick Strugnell**
**University of Melbourne,**
**Melbourne School of Graduate Research**

**David Beckett**
**University of Melbourne,**
**Melbourne School of Graduate Research**

There are currently multiple drivers for the development of national and international research and research training collaborations between institutional partners who may themselves be seen as 'equal' or 'unequal' with one another. Such drivers include i) the increasing 'globalization' of knowledge through an expanded internet, ii) increased participation in the generation of knowledge by less well-resourced communities, through international philanthropy and the use of technology, iii) the need to share expensive research infrastructure and expertise, iv) government-supported outreach and capacity-building, v) the expanded vision of young researchers beyond national and geographical boundaries, vi) the pursuit of research intensification as a marker of institutional status, and vii) the emergence of interdisciplinarity as a response to problems faced around the world, such as climate change. Such collaborations can be crystallized in the research training area in different ways, around short visits by researchers, extended student exchanges, and ultimately through enrolment in PhD degree programs in two (or potentially more) universities.

In addition to standard bilateral arrangements, university collectives such as Universitas 21 (U21), and, within Australia, the Group of Eight (Go8) research-intensive Universities, are developing regulatory frameworks that will facilitate access by candidates to Joint/Dual PhD programs within such collectives. Based on, albeit limited, experience, it appears that top-down, university-to-university agreements, which are typically MOU-based, are the most difficult to populate with candidates. In contrast, if there are two similar research loci in different universities where the Principal Investigators are in close contact, i.e. have a collaborative history and freely exchange research experiences, discuss their research outputs and, where appropriate, co-publish, then the placement of candidates into Dual or Joint programs often works very effectively. This 'bottom-up' approach is the one now favoured by the

University of Melbourne, and this paper elaborates on some of the details we encounter, using this approach.

Like many universities, Melbourne does not admit students into *Double Degree* PhD Programs – in such programs, the candidate is awarded two independent PhDs for the same body of work. Instead, Melbourne supports Joint PhDs (one testamur on graduation, two logos) or Dual degrees (two testamurs, both acknowledging the participation of the other university). At the operational level, the picture is much more complex and it is important to recognise these operational complexities at the outset, to avoid conflict that inevitably has an impact upon the candidate. The major issues include:

- Admissions standards
- Identifying the Lead/Home Institution
- Supervision/Mentoring/Advising
- Progression
- Examination
- Candidate support
- Intellectual Property
- Testamurs and use of the Titles

Each of these issues will be briefly addressed. Some can be managed very early through application or admission forms, i.e. by clearly documenting potential points of conflict, and working to resolve them amicably at the start.

## 1. Admissions Standards

The admissions standards for PhDs within Australia and especially within the Go8 share many similarities. These admission practices may vary from those in US or EU institutions. It is rare in Australia for candidates to be asked, for example, to provide a GRE score. Australian institutions usually require research experience, and performance in undergraduate programs and Master's level studies at a GPA of 3.0-3.5/4.0 is required. German students would require a GPA of 2.3 (i.e. using the German inverse GPA), whereas UK or Indian students are almost always required to have 'first class Honours' to be competitive for living stipends. Assessing equivalency of international and even national education standards is a problem that extends much beyond PhD admissions. Even within Australia there are differences – Queensland has a 7-point GPA and the awarding of 'distinctions' and 'high distinctions' is handled differently by Australian Universities, sometimes within the same state. Obviously, any student entering a Joint or Dual PhD Program must satisfy the entry requirements of both institutions and Melbourne considers each case on its merits.

## 2. Identifying the Lead Institution

In Melbourne's experience, it is important to designate one of the participating universities as the Lead Institution. In practice, candidates will spend the majority of their time at the Lead Institution. The Lead Institution will conduct the primary enrolment (though the candidate is enrolled in both Universities), ensure that the candidate has the necessary stipend support and other student support services (e.g., access to housing etc.), will carry greater responsibility for ensuring progress of the student, and provide the overarching regulatory framework within which the candidature will be conducted. Pragmatically, this means completion hurdles and timelines. The Lead Institution will usually also provide the student with a living stipend. The non-Lead institution may be described as the Host Institution (sometimes the Lead is called the Home Institution, though the terms "Home" and "Host" can be confusing, especially when translated from English into another language).

## 3. Supervision/Mentoring/Advising

There are surprising differences in the supervision models that exist globally. It is fundamental that the research conducted by every Joint/Dual PhD candidate is formally supervised and that a supervisor(s) is identified in each institution at point of enrolment, or earlier, at point of application. In the US, some responsibility for this task is delegated to an Advisory Committee; in Australia, the responsibility may rest with a single individual called the Primary Supervisor, who may be supported by co-supervisors and external supervisors, if there is extended field work, for example. It is important that sanctions can be applied to the Primary Supervisor for non-compliance with University policy and process. The Primary Supervisor in Australia may be line-managed by the Head of the enrolling Department or, in the case of some medical research, hold an adjunct (i.e. honorary) appointment with the enrolling Department. Regardless of the structure, it is essential that the candidate feels supported by an Advisor/Mentor in both institutions and that the supervisors discuss, and then agree, on the path that the candidate should follow. While they may, as is increasingly common, be from different disciplines, they must share a similar vision for the project that the candidate is tackling.

## 4.    Progression

Most Australian institutions enrol students into probationary candidature, or into convertible Master's by Research candidature where the candidature is 'upgraded' to a PhD on completion of Year 1 performance milestones. Near the end of Year 1, all candidates meet with an extended Advisory Committee and are assessed for their potential to complete their PhD. Sometimes the Committee will indicate that the probationary candidature be extended and create milestones that the candidate must hit in order to progress. Through the remainder of candidature there are annual reports filed by candidate and supervisor that provide information on the attainment of graduate attributes, and the level of resources available on the quality of supervision, and the level of endeavour displayed by the candidate. It is important that at least the Lead Institution has some form of 'active candidature' management process since the movement between facilities, and associated lag time and differential access to resources, can place pressure on a candidate's progress.

## 5.    Examination

The examination process of the typical 80-100k words thesis/dissertation must be agreed to at the commencement of candidature, or earlier, such as at point of application. Examination processes differ significantly in different jurisdictions. In Australia, the supervisor(s) suggests examiners but plays no part in the examination process. The Melbourne examination requires that the thesis be written in English, except in rare circumstances, and be read and scrutinised by two external examiners, where usually at least one of these examiners is from outside Australia. The use of international examiners has meant that the Australian examination process has evolved without an oral exam (i.e. *viva voce*) though most Australian candidates are asked to present a formal completion seminar where the central argument is outlined and any key data presented. In other systems, a *viva* is essential and in such circumstances, Melbourne will accept an oral examination, which is usually concluded over the internet using video conferencing. Regardless of the processes used, Melbourne requires that its examination standards are met and that the thesis is read and approved by two external examiners. Furthermore, both Universities must agree on 'process' details – such as whether a fail on the written document can be 'rescued' by an outstanding oral defence. The distribution of costs associated with the examination (such as travel to attend the *viva*), the final format of the dissertation, how many printed copies that are provided, whether a digital copy is to be submitted, and whether this digital copy is to be subject to electronic plagiarism software, should also be discussed and settled at the commencement of candidature or earlier.

## 6.   Candidate Support

Candidates must receive a living stipend and sufficient support to enable travel between the Lead and the Host institutions. Some candidates will attempt to obtain a living stipend from both the Lead and Host institutions. Melbourne usually resists this for two reasons. Firstly, PhD stipends are income tax-free in Australia; there is a limit on the additional stipend income a candidate can receive. In part this limit is imposed to preserve the tax-free nature of the stipend. Secondly, the driver for doing Joint/Dual degrees should not be financial, i.e. candidates should not participate simply because they receive twice the stipend. The extent of additional student supports will depend on the universities/countries involved and there is considerable variability in resources available, e.g., access to cheap housing between countries, cities and universities. Candidates should be covered for healthcare costs in both countries. In Australia, all domestic students are covered through a national health scheme, but this coverage will not usually extend to another country unless some specific arrangement is made. Like the other issues raised above, the arrangement should be captured on the early paperwork.

## 7.   Intellectual Property

The issue of IP is very complex, not the least because different universities have different rules regarding ownership of IP, and whether students do or do not own IP that comes from their project, and under what circumstances this IP is automatically, or through a physical deed, assigned to the university or some other stakeholder (e.g. grant provider). The intrinsic complexity of IP ownership where two parties are involved can be compounded where there is a dispute over which University has made the major contribution, intellectually, or through financial resources or access to background IP. It is important therefore to establish, in prospect, the arrangements for sharing (and paying for) the IP that might be generated from a Joint/Dual PhD Project. Ideally, 'shared' students should not commence projects that target the generation of IP though it is recognised that all projects in some areas have the potential to develop valuable IP. Regardless, the research supervisors must discuss IP and IP arrangements openly with candidates and must take on the responsibility for ensuring that IP issues do not impact adversely on the candidature.

## 8.   Testamurs and the Use of the Degree Title

All universities provide completing PhD candidates with a formal document, sometimes called a parchment or testamur. The testamur typically carries the granting university's crest, at least the title of the degree and the name of the candidate, and signatures from officers of the university. Some countries have very specific rules regarding the testamur and preclude the addition of another university crest; in such circumstances the candidate would enrol in a Dual PhD degree. In a Joint degree, where both logos are present, the testamur should describe that the PhD was granted for studies conducted within, and under the supervision of, both institutions. In Dual PhDs, the testamur should reference the fact that the other university was involved in the research and supervision of the candidate. While there appear to be few conventions regarding how granted degrees appear, Melbourne supports the convention of: *Mary Brown PhD (Melb & UBC)*, rather than *Mary Brown PhD (Melb) PhD (UBC)*, which implies a double degree.

## Conclusion

This paper has focussed on the technical aspects of Joint/Dual degree administration. The complexity of processes suggests that they should not be entered into lightly. As important and as testing as these operational issues can be, it is fundamental that all parties establish why a Dual/Joint Program is important for a specific candidature, and ensure that the relevant key driver(s) are manifest in the training provided. For example, if the aim is capacity-building, then the research training provided must not be contingent on equipment that can never be accessed in the less well-resourced environment. By the same token, there should be a discussion with the candidate about the period beyond completion, early in the degree, to ensure that there is a commitment to return to the home country if that is a driver. Most importantly, where supervision is shared (as it typically is under both Dual and Joint candidatures), academic expertise should be made explicitly relevant, available and well-understood by all who participate. People should know what, and with whom, they are signing on to do! This is because intrinsic issues that result in poor completion rates in PhDs conducted at single institutions would appear to be compounded by asking a candidate to complete in two different environments in a Joint/Dual PhD Program. This should be borne in mind when candidates indicate that they favour a Joint/Dual degree, and the issues explored and explained to potential supervisors and candidates alike.

However, the benefits of shrinking and linking the global research community, and the use of PhD candidates as the 'glue' to join appropriate research activities and researchers in different countries, has considerable appeal, and every attempt should be made to support this type of activity, once the risks are explained and the 'bottom-up' enthusiasm for such candidatures is clearly demonstrated in ways we have outlined here.

# European Collaboration in Master's and Doctoral Programmes

## Jean Chambaz
## Université Pierre et Marie Curie

European universities have been engaged in setting up joint programmes for a number of years and still display considerable interest in engaging in this type of collaboration. The European Union funding schemes have supported such activities for a number of political and ideological reasons, such as furthering mobility and creating a European identity. Indeed, the benefits of creating joint programmes are numerous for both the universities as well as for students and society at large. For this reason the European ministers for higher education have explicitly called joint programmes a "Hallmark of the European Higher Education Area" in a statement from 2003.[1] In 2009 they repeated the importance of mobility and set the very ambitious target that 20 % of all European graduates should have had a mobility experience by 2020.

The joint programmes have been most numerous on the Master's level on the three-cycle Bologna structure (Bachelor's, Master's and Doctoral cycle), as the students at this level are seen to have the maturity to benefit from the international experience. It is essential to keep in mind here that the term "graduate student" is rarely compatible with the European system. Master's and doctoral programmes are—except in Britain and a few other countries —kept strictly apart not only institutionally, but also in the academic culture and, not least, in terms of employment contracts. Given the albeit slow trend in Europe towards giving doctoral candidates status as employees, and the much stronger, parallel trend towards viewing doctoral education as being qualitatively different from the first and second cycle, the independent status of the doctorate is unlikely to change.

On the Master's level, the discussion about joint programmes has been very much connected to the general topics of the Bologna Process; comparability, recognition, quality assurance and learning outcomes have all been important issues. As the European University Association underlined in its 2006 report *Quality Enhancement in European Master's Programmes*, a "culture of jointness" is essential to successful programmes: the programme should be more than the sum of its parts, while building on common ideas, transparent procedures as well as curiosity and trust. The emphasis on these

---

1   Recommendations from the Berlin Conference of European Higher Education Ministers, 19 September 2003.

elements is not least due to the diversity of Master's programmes, which vary considerably across academic cultures and national education systems. These differences require that there exist a very high degree of "jointness" and integration in terms of curriculum and assessment. The content of the courses and the assessment have to be very well coordinated and integrated in the common understanding of the programme and the common understanding of quality.

While doctoral education is part of the Bologna process as well, the issues need to be understood differently than on the Master's level. The gradual progress from course-based learning to research that happens in graduate education in the US sense is much more abrupt in most of Europe. Doctoral candidates (the European term for graduate students) will enter the programme and often a new institutional setting in the doctoral school with a research project. In many disciplines, they will be expected to embark on their research from the first day with very few courses; they will be seen as an individual junior member faculty member and not part of a cohort. This means that there is little sense of belonging to a 'class' that goes through a shared curriculum. As a consequence, the important issues concerning joint Master's are of less concern. Instead of a learning environment (in the strictest sense), the doctoral candidates are part of a research environment, where they need exposure to the research community. The very individual trajectories mean that the kind of integration of curriculum that is characteristic of joint Master's is much less relevant for mobility in doctoral education. Rather, the central concern is to expose the doctoral candidates to the international research community in a way that makes sense for the individual research project and researcher profile.

From one perspective, some of the issues concerning the 'jointness' of collaborations are less difficult in doctoral education. Good research is international by nature, and good local research environments will be part of larger formal or informal international communities and networks that do have a joint understanding of the discipline. The problems related to assessment and courses will be much less relevant for mobility within such communities. In this sense, the existing networks will already have a "culture of jointness." However, these networks are often dependent on personal contacts and risk being unrelated to the longer term strategies of the institution. Developing institutionalised possibilities for mobility based on these networks require an institutional framework to assure sustainability, openness and transparency of the collaboration. There is a need for interplay between the bottom-up approach that builds on the research environment and the top-down approach of structures and strategic planning for and by the institution.

From the perspective of the doctoral candidate, it is important that the programme be an encouraged possibility, but it also has to make sense for the individual research project. Very rigid and standardised mobility requirements may be seen as a guarantee for the international element, but the added value can just as well be diminished if mobility prolongs time to degree. Again, this issue marks the difference between joint doctoral and joint Master's programmes, since the latter can proscribe a specific, pre-determined mobility experience due to the cumulative, cohort-based nature of the Master. However, if there is a large degree of individual discretion towards mobility in a joint doctoral programme, how should this mobility be structured, assessed and certified?

There has been no clear answer to this question in Europe. EU funding, particularly through the Erasmus Mundus programme, explicitly promotes integrated structures so that mobility is not a simple 'add-on' to the research project and so that institutions can ensure that the role of the participating institutions clearly complement each other. Here, the programme must also award a joint or dual degree. While this approach is very transparent in terms of what kind of mobility is undertaken and how it relates to the desired outcomes of the programme, it risks putting too large an administrative burden on the partner institutions while not being flexible enough to accommodate the individual needs of doctoral candidates. At the other end of the spectrum, some universities offer a range of individual arrangements that give the individual doctoral candidate more freedom, but without imposing a very structured relationship between these arrangements and the programme. In fact, the university might simply take note of a mobility experience without linking it to a specific structure or programme, and then create a certificate or supplement to the diploma that recognizes the mobility experience. While this practice does have the flexibility needed for learning through research, it lacks the transparency of the integrated model, and the certificate will often have an unclear legal status.

It thus seems that the European move towards more structured doctoral education with clear institutional strategies will also create more diverse and more clearly profiled collaborations between different institutions, from the integrated degree-awarding programme to the individual certification of mobility experiences by a single university.

# Joint and Dual Degree Programs at the University of Arizona

**Andrew Comrie**
**University of Arizona**

**Dianne D. Horgan**
**University of Arizona**

Joint and dual graduate degree programs enable students, faculty members and universities to benefit from the expanded opportunities available among the participating programs and institutions. The formal structures of these degree programs are embodied in similar administrative mechanisms that articulate and coordinate the academic components of the collaboration to meet the needs and requirements of all the participants.

## Conceptual Structure

It is important to note that, conceptually, joint and dual degrees are not fundamentally different from other kinds of degrees, whether they be international partnerships, domestic multi-university collaborations, dual programs within a single university, or even a standard single-program degree. There is generally no need to invent a separate conceptual model for international joint and dual degree programs. Rather, joint and dual degree programs are conceptually and structurally similar to other degrees, and therefore they can be implemented using existing policies and practices.

The conceptual structure of a regular single-major graduate degree program offered at one university has several building blocks. There are two of these that are primary in the U.S. context, a coursework component and an experiential component. In the U.S. there is a long history of advanced coursework at the graduate level, which is paired with experiential learning aimed most often at scholarship in research and creativity, in the form of a thesis or dissertation. The former component provides breadth, and the latter depth as well as integration. Other forms of experiential components are used, the most prominent being in professional degree programs in which a report on an applied project, internship or service experience is produced instead. In the U.S. and elsewhere, the relative weight of these primary components can vary from thesis-only degrees to programs made up exclusively of coursework.

Graduate degree structures usually also contain a range of secondary building blocks that vary by field and purpose. These can include components representing a minor disciplinary concentration, methodology and techniques, clinical experience, thematic elective courses, and more. Most individual programs encode these primary and secondary components within the formal requirements for the major and the degree. These requirements are typically most extensive for the doctorate, moderately so for a master's degree, and least extensive for graduate certificates. Certification that a student has completed a particular course of study is provided by two documents, the detailed official transcript and the final diploma with appropriate seals and signatures.

When we consider all the forms of a graduate degree, these building blocks must be kept in mind. Joint and dual degrees (and certificates) are essentially achieving the same ends, but with two or more programs agreeing to provide different components or different parts thereof in order to create a whole degree, whether within the same university, between domestic institutions, or internationally.

## Definitions and Characteristics

At the University of Arizona (UA), our use of "dual" and "joint" degree closely follows definitions articulated by CGS[1]:

- Dual degree programs are formal programs that result in the awarding of *two degrees*. Typically there is some overlap so that the total number of units required is reduced. Because the degrees already exist at our university, we can approve these internally without Board approval. The Graduate Council approved guidelines for the amount of double-counting we will accept. So as long as proposed dual degree programs fall within the pre-approved parameters,[2] the Graduate College can approve dual degrees. For dual degrees with other institutions, we follow the logic of our internal dual degrees: Students must be accepted in each program and must meet all the requirements for each degree. At least 50% percent of each degree must be unique. We treat coursework from the other university as transfer credit. We create a Memorandum of Understanding with the partner university, guaranteeing that we will accept their transfer

---

[1]  *The Graduate International Collaborations Project: A North American Perspective on Joint and Dual Degree Programs,* Daniel Denecke and Julia Kent. *CGS Communicator,* Volume 42, No. 8, October 2009.

[2]  Details can be found online http://oirps.arizona.edu/CURRICULUM/HTML/dual.html

work. We charge regular tuition and follow our usual policies and procedures.

- At the University of Arizona, joint degrees are formal programs whereby students earn a *single degree, but with two majors*. The UA often accomplishes the same goal through interdisciplinary majors and minors as well as graduate certificates. Since these are essentially new degrees, they require full internal and Board approval. While we have joint degrees with our sister institution, Arizona State University, we do not offer joint degrees with foreign universities. We do, however, offer joint *programs*. These are cooperative arrangements whereby we share resources with another university. In our Transcultural German Ph.D. program with Leipzig University,[3] UA students spend one year at Leipzig and German students spend one year at UA; students receive only one degree from their home institution.

Students cannot 'invent' their own dual degree programs, but they may take a concurrent or second degree. *Concurrent or second degrees* are structures that allow a student to enroll in two programs, either concurrently or sequentially. There does not have to be a formal program that links the two degrees. For example, a student may earn an MBA and then decide to become a teacher and earn an M.Ed. If some course work can legitimately apply to both degrees, students may 'double count' up to 20% of the required coursework (i.e., 6 hrs for a 30 hour master's degree). A second Ph.D. requires Graduate College approval. Recent changes to Graduate College Policy allow students with foreign Ph.D.s to apply for a second U.S. Ph.D.

We offer a number of Graduate Certificates[4] which, following CGS,[5] we define as a linked series of credit-bearing graduate courses that constitute a coherent body of knowledge. These are, in theory, available to international students, but in order to qualify for an F-1 visa, students must be able to take at least 9 credits (fulltime status) in their first semester. Since certificates are usually 12-15 credits, it is rare that there are sufficient courses available per semester. Only a handful of our certificates meet this requirement. We are adding more online certificates that often show strong international enrollment. The faculty is developing certificates that lead to contracts to train international

---

3    Further information can be found online at http://grad.arizona.edu/live/programs/description/181

4    See online for additional details at http://oirps.arizona.edu/CURRICULUM/HTML/certdev.html

5    Post-Baccalaureate Certificates: A First Look at Graduate Certificate Programs offered by CGS Member Institutions, Stephen Welch and Peter Syverson, *CGS Communicator*, Council of Graduate Schools, Washington, DC, Vol. XXX, No. 9, November 1997.

students, such as our just-approved certificate to provide advanced training to Saudi pharmacists. We find many employers and foreign governments eager to fund graduate certificates. We have identified an additional practical issue with regard to visas: it is advisable to avoid having students do year one, two and three in different places, because they have to obtain new documents each time they move from one campus to the next.

## Discussion

Our strategy for developing these avenues for international collaboration has been first to develop clear guidelines for collaborative programs within our own university. We try to maintain consistency among our policies for internal and external dual degrees and second graduate degrees. Then we extend to international partners, choosing partners whose reputations will enhance or extend our own. As much as possible, we use our existing programs and policies, thus avoiding many of the stumbling blocks. We charge our regular tuition, use our usual transfer credit policies, follow our own policies on double-counting of credit, and let the partner institution control their own degree.

As research has become increasingly interdisciplinary and collaborative, we have quite naturally re-assessed our position on theses and dissertations. We no longer accept the single-authored study as the only model. We allow students working together in labs to submit shared dissertations with each student identifying their own unique contributions. Once we accepted that model, it became clear that one thesis or one dissertation for two degrees can be justified as long as the student clearly identifies the unique contribution to each degree and that the work has sufficient breadth for both degrees. We already allow special members from other universities to serve on committees, so having committees from two UA departments or from a UA department and another university was an easy extension.

Another avenue we are pursuing is an extension of our Accelerated Master's programs.[6] In these arrangements, top students can simultaneously finish their undergraduate degree and work toward a master's degree. We believe extending this to international students will be a way to deal with the problem of whether or not to admit students with 3-year bachelor's degrees.

In short, we see our international dual degrees as a logical expansion of the collaborative work we have already done within our university and with scholars from other universities. We also see certificates and dual degrees

---

6  See details online at http://oirps.arizona.edu/CURRICULUM/Accelerated_Masters_Program_ Proposal.html

as a way to deal with other collaboration issues. Like many universities, we have a number of 'informal' research collaborations that fly "under the radar," presenting all sorts of potential liability problems. These can include students who are on campus and in labs informally, paying no tuition yet using resources. We find that by offering them something of value such as an additional degree or certificate, we can bring them into the system.

Universities are often seen as rigid bureaucracies. Yet, operating within our own policies and by approving overall guidelines for certificates, dual degrees, and other programs, we can fairly easily encourage and accommodate international collaborations and partnerships.

*Note: Andrew C. Comrie, Ph.D. and Dianne D. Horgan, Ph.D. are, respectively, Dean and Associate Dean of the Graduate College at the University of Arizona.*

# Joint and Dual Programs: Reconciling North American Customs with International Opportunities

## Douglas M. Peers
## York University

Interest in international collaborative programming at the graduate level has exploded over the past decade. Triggered by the reimagining and restructuring of post-secondary education in Europe associated with the Bologna Accords, fueled by the expansion and diversification of university education in Asia and Latin America, driven by the increasing demand for Master's-level credentials within most post-industrial economies, and framed by the increasingly global flow of ideas and individuals, Canadian and American universities are under growing pressures to rethink graduate education, particularly at the Master's level. We are moreover subject to contradictory pressures. On the one hand, there is increasing recognition of the value of greater cooperation and collaboration between institutions and between countries. Yet universities are locked into intense competition with one another to secure top students for their programs. And finally, notwithstanding the many reservations expressed to date about the merits and accuracy of the various university ranking systems in play, nobody can deny that the privileged position hitherto enjoyed by Anglophone universities is no longer assured. Nor is it realistic or even desirable to assume that this status could or should be restored.

Clear proof of the changes underway is the surge in interest in joint and/or dual degrees, including cotutelles, most notably at the Master's level. European universities, with the possible exception of many in the UK, are keenly pursuing potential partners. Demand is partly rooted in the commitment within the Bologna process to encourage student mobility, a commitment increasingly difficult to satisfy at the level of the baccalaureate. As many European countries move towards three-year baccalaureates, their universities find there is not enough time to accommodate extended periods of academic exchange in what is often a very packed and relatively inflexible curriculum. This has in turn led European universities to shift their mobility focus to the master's degree. European students are also eager for North American credentials and experience and here their desire has been reinforced no doubt by the fact that the Master's degree is becoming the entry-level requirement for many careers. And finally, some faculty have come to value how such collaborative programming can buttress their own research undertakings.

Anecdotal evidence from recent trips to Europe suggests that there seems to be a preference for dual degrees at the Master's level. While there appears to be some fuzziness about what differentiates a joint degree from a dual degree, one generally agreed-upon distinction is that a joint degree produces a single degree certificate and is based upon an integrated curriculum that is mutually developed by the two partners. A dual degree, on the other hand, produces two degree certificates and does not require the same level of curricular planning and integration. At the doctoral level, there appears to be less interest in or even an appetite for collaborative degrees save for what might be arranged for an individual student. Doctoral education remains very individualized and in many cases there is no core curriculum or required courses that could be developed and/or shared between institutions. Hence, it is more difficult to conceive of more generalized dual PhD degree programs. However, there is a growing recognition that some students may benefit from a customized collaborative program that addresses their research programs and to that end, a number of universities are beginning to experiment with cotutelles with varying degrees of enthusiasm.

Arguably, joint degrees are the easiest to defend on academic and pedagogical grounds. Both partners, at least in theory, work together to develop a curriculum that draws on what each can do best so as to create an integrated and in some cases an innovative collaborative program of study. Moreover, as joint degrees result in only one degree certificate, their proponents can avoid often contentious questions about giving students the opportunity to count some of their courses towards more than one degree ('double-dipping'), questions that are frequently raised when dual degrees are brought forward. But in practice joint degrees are much more difficult to develop. Beyond the added costs and logistical challenges of moving people about in some kind of synchronized order, there are procedural challenges. Joint degrees are generally subject to a much higher level of scrutiny within each institution's administrative system as each partner has to work at ensuring compatibility of the degree with their own internal requirements. There is the added challenge that joint degrees pose to the various accreditation/quality assurance processes in place. For example, in evaluating the competencies of faculty associated with the program, how does an accreditation board or quality assurance agency in one jurisdiction address faculty in another? Similar questions emerge when issues of student admission, registration, and support are raised. The legal status of graduate students does vary between jurisdictions and this can lead to difficult issues. For example, if a program is jointly administered by two institutions with the students in effect "belonging to both," which institution's (or for that matter which government's) understanding and application of intellectual property law or research ethics applies? There is also the spectre of students sitting in the same program, for which they will receive the same degree, yet with some enjoying a higher level of funding or a lower tuition fee. A truly joint degree makes it more difficult to justify the presence or persistence of differential treatments amongst the students.

Not surprisingly, the impression gleaned from the discussions that I and others have had with European universities is that they are more interested in dual degrees than in joint degrees: in part this is the result of the difficulties noted above. I suspect that North American universities will also prove to be more receptive to dual degrees, notwithstanding their reservations over 'double-dipping,' which I will address later. It is also important to note that joint degrees do not deliver what European students seem to want most of all: a North American degree in addition to a European degree, which is what a dual degree offers.

Dual degrees have the advantage of avoiding at least some of the curricular challenges noted above. In most cases, they consist of some form of advanced credit or transfer credit system such that students are able to acquire two degrees by drawing on courses offered at two institutions. As the degrees are usually already in existence, there is no need to develop new programs or add new courses, and hence they can more quickly secure institutional and external approvals. Dual degrees are less likely to be bedeviled by procedural wranglings over quality assurance. Each of the two degrees that comprise the dual degree remains subject to the respective accreditation or quality assurance body governing that degree.

The biggest obstacle facing many of us who implement dual degrees is one that is firmly anchored in current academic culture. While European universities seem to be relatively untroubled by what is often negatively described in North America as "double-dipping," a survey of colleagues on this side of the Atlantic suggests that institutional governing bodies (senates, faculty councils, etc.) are often reluctant to grant what they see as two degrees for 'work' that would otherwise only result in a single degree. In some instances this can be addressed by adjusting requirements such that students are expected to undertake more work than would normally result in just a single degree. While this is an option that some institutions have introduced, in some instances it was done more to head off complaints about 'double dipping' than it was to fulfill the programmatic objectives of the program of study. As long as we continue to obsess about courses and define a degree in terms of its inputs (number of credits, number of courses, number of terms) rather than its outputs (anticipated outcomes in terms of skills learned, research undertaken, exposure to new ideas or methodologies, etc.), we will continue to encounter stiff resistance to dual degrees.

The Bologna process has opened up possibilities in Europe that have enabled some universities there to think more creatively about degree standards and nomenclature. There are moves being made in a number of institutions to operationalize one of the foundational elements in the Bologna accord, namely a shift towards understanding and defining a degree in terms of outputs. Their emphasis is increasingly upon defining degree expectations in terms of the skills/knowledge/experiences a student has achieved at the conclusion of the degree. Framed in those terms, a dual degree becomes more defensible, not to mention comprehensible, as it recognizes that a student has experienced something substantively different from and greater than that which they would have gained from a single degree taken at any one institution. And if we take into account the rather bewildering and inconsistent definition and/or understanding of what constitutes a master's degree – some are one year in length, others may be two years in length, some require a substantial original piece of research, others are largely course-based, yet all often result in a master's degree that commonly is either presented as a Master of Arts or a Master of Science— an unhelpful fixation on inputs (or fetishization of credits) becomes even more indefensible.

The issue of joint and/or dual degrees at the doctoral level has excited comparatively less attention. One exception is the cotutelle wherein a student is co-supervised by faculty from two different institutions, and upon completion is either awarded a degree certificate noting both institutions, or may receive two degrees with some kind of notification, perhaps on the transcripts, that the student's program of study was undertaken in a cotutelle environment. Cotutelles are particularly popular in France, and interest in them is growing in Australia. In Canada, they are most commonly found in Quebec though a number of institutions in Ontario are beginning to experiment with them. Our experience to date has been somewhat limited, though early signs are very promising. A lot of work is required for what in effect is an individualized doctoral program. But because they operate at an individual level, they do not need the kinds of institutional approvals that a collaborative program requires. They appear to work best when initiated by two researchers who are already collaborating and who can provide the appropriate environments in which the student can benefit. Cotutelles also appear to fit more naturally within the sciences where collaborative research is already the norm, and there are visible and tangible benefits to students who have access to the facilities and research teams at more than one institution.

Some institutions have introduced templates to regularize cotutelle relationships. York University chose instead to develop a checklist as we found that no single template could encompass the requirements and/or expectations that arise when cotutelles are being arranged with a variety of institutions. At York, students registering in a cotutelle are expected to meet the requirements of both programs. This means, for example, that in the case of a cotutelle arranged with a European partner, the student would be required to complete the coursework expected in a North American PhD. The checklist also requires that regulations governing intellectual property, ethics, arrangements for funding, the number of terms to be spent at each institution, and other requirements are clearly and transparently articulated at the very outset. As we have had only limited experience to date with cotutelles, we also decided upon a checklist rather than a template as it is easier to revise a checklist than it is to amend a template.

There is no doubt that graduate deans are often perched precariously on the shifting frontiers of an increasingly globalized academic world and it is very easy to become seduced by the siren calls of collaborative programming. Joint, dual and cotutelle degrees hold out many temptations. But enthusiasm for them is far from certain on many of our campuses. While few today would decry efforts at internationalization, we have not fully thought through the current administrative, cultural, and political obstacles that lay before us. And ironically, resistance is often most stridently expressed by faculty members who see dual degrees as cheapening the value of a graduate degree, turning it into a commodity that is increasingly driven by demand for credentials rather than knowledge. Their fears are not without some merit, even if the rhetoric leans towards pious and nostalgic invocations of the good old days (usually defined as the period when they were in graduate school). They are however correct in drawing attention to the dangers of becoming too market-driven. We can best avoid this pitfall if we uphold the purposes of graduate education, but focus our understanding of it in such a way as to think about the outcomes of that education rather than simply the inputs provided for it. Collaborative degrees offer potentially valuable learning experiences for our students, and may also provide further opportunities for inter-institutional collaboration that will benefit the wider university community.

# Preparing Students for Supervised Research in an International Context: Etiquette and Ethics

### Sheila Bonde
### Brown University

Preparing students to do research in an international setting requires a number of factors. From a long list, I would first signal: curiosity. Students need to be encouraged to pursue study abroad out of genuine intellectual and cultural interest in situations different from their own. Support for students experiencing new and different situations, however, can be undervalued, especially at the graduate level. Stipend amounts, availability of housing, and the presence of adequate medical and mental health support services, is often not fully considered. In order to profit from study abroad, language training is also essential. Although students in our new exchange program in mathematics assure me that "we all speak math," deep knowledge about each other's verbal languages is also helpful! Along with language preparation should also come training in cultural sensitivity. This needs to involve what I call "etiquette" as well as ethics. On the etiquette side come questions of social interaction: how to behave in class, when to shake hands, or how to disagree politely in the host culture. On the ethical side come questions of awareness: how to be aware of global problems and how to find ways to solve them for the good of all.

Brown University's international programs are varied in structure and put a focus upon opportunities for student research and training, rather than curricular offerings. For example, students can participate in the Brown—Paris VI program in Mathematics and Applied Mathematics. In this program, dissertation projects for advanced doctoral students are co-advised by faculty members from both institutions. The students from Paris spend at least a semester at Brown, while our students spend a semester or year in Paris. Many of our international programs are designed to foster undergraduate study, graduate and faculty research, depending upon the need and current projects. For example, our exchange agreement with the Chinese University of Hong Kong permits students to attend the host institution for a semester, funded by their "home" institution. A student in our master's program in public humanities recently attended for a semester to study and to participate in theatrical performance. Other exchange programs foster training opportunities. Our exchange program with Makerere University in Uganda brings public health trainees to Brown to experience top of the line facilities, and sends Brown students to gain experience in HIV-AIDS clinics. Other exchange relationships exist simply to accommodate the occasional researcher, at the faculty or graduate student level. Students normally visit for a semester in order to accomplish research related to their dissertations.

In all of these endeavors, one of our concerns has been ethical training for our students. A recently-awarded grant from the National Science Foundation is helping us to confront the cultural context of ethical decision-making while students are studying abroad, or while students from international institutions are visiting at Brown. This project, titled, "*Ethical Awareness in International Collaborations: A Contextual Approach*," is developing a training module for graduate students launching fieldwork projects, collaborative international partnerships or community-based partnerships with diverse populations. In all these endeavors, graduate students must be aware of cultural values that may be different than their own.

Scholarly integrity is recognized as an important issue in scientific research and training. Yet there are profound differences in the larger cultural context for ethical decision-making. As international collaborations become more common, these differences need to be confronted. Training in the Responsible Conduct of Research tends to ignore the cross-cultural challenges of ethical decision-making. Instead, RCR instruction has largely been proscriptive, field- and country-specific, and universalizing, based on fundamentally western notions of individual intellectual property rights rather than collaborative values. This project instead puts its emphasis upon cultural context and upon partnership with international scholars and diverse community groups in developing a new kind of training in scholarly integrity. The project is itself a partnership, and fosters discussion of ethical values across international and cultural boundaries. Researchers at Brown University are working with collaborators at the Indian Institute for Technology and Zhejiang University in China. The final results of this project will include: a research paper discussing the formation of the physical science disciplines of physics, chemistry and engineering, and the impact of that discipline formation on ethic decision-making; a case-study-based curriculum developed in collaboration with our international partners; a research paper on the curriculum design and its assessment module; and a web site dedicated to making these resources broadly available.

This year, the Graduate School at Brown is hosting a faculty-graduate student workshop to gather information on international ethics training and scholarship in other countries. Researchers (graduate students and faculty) in STEM fields, and in the fields of philosophy, educational policy, science studies, legal studies and anthropology come together every other week to explore the factors that enable or inhibit cross-cultural ethical understanding. These scholars are contributing their expertise in forging policy decisions, in negotiating varying definitions of ethics, and in understanding fieldwork contexts. The workshop is helping to define points of similarity and difference in approaches to scholarly integrity, and is assembling case study examples. We are meeting by teleconference and Skype with our partners at the Indian Institute for Technology (in Mumbai, India) and Zhejiang University (in China), and this spring, our partners visited Brown to attend at least one workshop. Next year, we will use the case studies identified in the first-year workshop to launch a pilot seminar course: *Scholarly Integrity in Fieldwork and International Collaborations.* This seminar will be co-located at Brown and at Zhejiang University and the Indian Institute. We will test the appropriateness of the case studies and will also pilot an assessment program to test the efficacy of the training modules. In the final year of the project, we will establish the seminar as a regular part of the Brown, Zhejiang and Mumbai curricula, and will publish a print and web-based brochure, making the approach available beyond the three campuses where they were developed.

The assessment of quality for many study abroad programs often resides principally in student satisfaction with the experience. Our project provides a model for training students, giving them the tools to face global problems within a cultural context. It places the emphasis beyond student satisfaction to preparedness in cultural literacy.

# International Joint Research in Academia: Supporting Foreign Students and Faculty

## Hasuck Kim
## Seoul National University

The two most valued key words in the academic community in recent years, perhaps, are interdisciplinary collaboration and internationalization. The first issue is originated from the current complex and urgent issues such as energy problems, climate change, environmental pollutions, and world food shortage, to name a few. The second issue naturally came from the fact that we are living in an increasingly globalized world where the meaning of national boundaries is far less clear than it used to be. Let's consider an example of the energy problem, which is not a local problem as it used to be. It is so important that all nations should be involved to solve these issues.

An example of an area that requires international collaboration is in the production and use of hydrogen, which is well-accepted as a key source of energy for the next centuries. Hydrogen provides great advantages such as abundant supply—there is no worry about the resource—and it produces water, a clean end-product; this is an environmentally benign cycle of energy use. An additional merit is that no carbon dioxide emission, which is believed a major source for the global warming and weather change, results. At the moment, however, the production cost for hydrogen exceeds that required for any other fuel. For this reason, we should find economically reasonable ways to produce, store, transport, and use hydrogen as a fuel. It takes chemists, physicists, material engineers, chemical engineers and mechanical engineers to accomplish this goal. It is quite obvious that energy problems will require international collaboration across many different disciplines.

In academia, internationalization leads to an influx of foreign people, professors as well as students. Each institute must be willing to be involved with international collaboration and prepare to accept those from overseas with different backgrounds and different languages in diverse academic trainings. International reputation is an undeniable component of today's world-class universities. The international migration of students and faculty is a major trend in higher education and is inevitably driven by globalization. The more negative concept of "brain drain" may be observed in certain places in some circumstances, but in the long run, the more positive idea of "brain circulation" will be borne out, since many researchers are seeking international opportunities that improve training and efficiency. To encourage this process at Seoul National University, we have adopted the following policies and practices to support foreign students and faculty.

For students, we are accepting applications every day for admission for both semesters. In addition, we set up interviews (site visits or by web-cam) with student candidates before they are finally accepted. In the interview, we check the level of preparation and their willingness to study in a given field. Then, our Office of International Affairs takes over to organize trips to the campus for admitted students. Another route for students in the group is through a joint international project. Faculty members from both institutes perform a joint project through respective funding agencies. Then their students visit the counterpart laboratory for a short time, or for a year, for research. This may lead to a dual degree or joint degree program between two institutes. This is a very natural way of creating international cooperation between Universities. We offer various scholarship programs for better students: the SNU Glo-harmony Program, the Silk Road Scholarship Program, the Graduate Scholarship for Foreign Students Program, and the Language Training Program for Asian Students (mainly for Mongolia, Vietnam, China and Sakhalin)

Faculty members are recommended by individual departments based on their academic excellence and personal character. Sometimes, it is necessary to provide extra financial incentives to recruit foreign professors. We offer a start-up fund, a special fund for exceptional cases from the President's office, to cover moving expenses, and provide university housing. We also provide support for the education for their children.

In the area of campus life, foreign students participate in a language course and activities to learn more about Korean culture. Fellow students in their class and/or in their research group provide support for daily life, coursework, and laboratory experiments. Most foreign students stay in the campus dormitories. Fellow members from each foreign country have their own student group and organize their own activities such as music performances and sports games. and exchange information about schooling and extracurricular activities.

For faculty members, one graduate student is assigned to each foreign faculty member in the department to help the faculty member. The assigned student may act as an assistant including interpretation if needed. Lectures are given in English and the lecture materials are available on the web for further study.

In addition, SNU requires that all official documents be made available to foreign vistors on the campus; therefore we make the English version of official documents for foreigners. An English handbook for foreign professors was prepared, which contains all necessary information about the university regulations including promotion, re-appointment, applications for research funds, classroom management and other issues. We also operate a Global Information Center where all information about on/off campus life can be obtained. It was also important to establish an English version of academic administrative information on the web, a resource that covers names of students taking courses, the lecture schedule, and the credits offered and roster. For faculty, we also provide information about year-end income tax calculations and salary statements. This resource is also useful for students in adding or dropping courses, applying for scholarships, registering, applying for a dormitory room, and reviewing curricula.

To prepare foreign students and faculty for their experiences on our campus, we hold a foreign faculty/student orientation each semester to hear their concerns and suggestions. During this period, we offer special occasions to explore Korean culture during one weekend. In the future we are planning to hire a foreign professor as a Vice-Dean of the Graduate School and a foreign staff to handle other important issues related to this event.

Since our university is in the beginning stages of extended globalization, there are many things to be done to improve the stay of foreign members in the campus. It was not easy because most staff members are not ready to communicate in English with them. We are still in the learning stage of full globalization. Collaboration requires the proper atmosphere and consensus among campus members, as well as an extra budget. Taking into consideration these factors will ensure that we build the resources necessary for "brain gain" and the sustainability of programs that encourage collaboration.

# A Model for Graduate Program Development: Study Abroad Programs at the College at Brockport, State University of New York

**Susan Stites-Doe**
**The College at Brockport, State University of New York**

**Ralph Trecartin**
**The College at Brockport, State University of New York**

## Background

The College at Brockport, State University of New York, is a comprehensive college located in the rural Western New York region between Buffalo, New York and Rochester, New York. In the fall of 2009 graduate enrollments numbered 1370. About 75% of our students take one or two classes a semester, and most take courses in the summer and winter intersession months. We offer 41 graduate programs, and the lion's share of our program offerings culminate with the earning of a Master's degree. Certificate programs, and combined degree programs that permit undergraduate students the opportunity to get a head start on a graduate degree are also part of our portfolio. The most heavily populated graduate programs are in Education fields. The campus also has growing Accounting, Public Administration, Professional Science Master's, and Physical Education programs, among others.

In any given year, 1-5% of SUNY Brockport's enrolled graduate students come to us from international locations. At present, most of our international students come from Canada. It is noteworthy that the Canadian border sits only some two hours to the north of the Brockport campus, and if one were to be able to follow a crow as it flies, one need only to fly directly across one of America's Great Lakes, Lake Ontario, to reach Canadian soil and arrive in the Province of Ontario, Canada.

## International Programs at The College at Brockport

For a myriad of reasons related to our campus mission, we have an interest in increasing the numbers of international students who apply to our graduate programs, and who later enroll in them. We also want to increase the numbers and types of international education programs that we make available to all students, undergraduate and graduate alike. It is our contention that becoming involved in the international global community is a good thing for our students, our faculty, and the campus community at large. We believe that students' diverse international experiences are life-changing and that we should encourage them to become conversant in the needs and conditions of the world beyond the State University of New York and their own home towns. We believe that by sending students out into the world to attend college programs offered in international locations, we not only enrich the traveling students' experiences directly, but also expand our campus's reputation and encourage international students in other countries to consider coming to Brockport to study with us. Thus, study abroad students are appreciated as ambassadors to The College at Brockport, and we view their role to be important to helping us achieve our mission as an institution of higher learning.

The College at Brockport has a rich history in Study abroad programs, having started in this arena with student exchange programs in the early 1960's. Early student exchanges were normally made for a period of one year and programs focused on individual study areas, e.g., foreign language. When conditions on college campuses across the United States changed, necessitating budget-balancing, study abroad programs began to supplant and supplement exchange programs. Study abroad programs such as ours were encouraged to begin operating as free-standing cost-centers. Study abroad programs are distinguished by the length of time of the study period and by the flexibility with which students may employ study credits at their home institutions. In such programs, students tend to study in another country for a maximum of one semester instead of over longer periods of time. This shortened time period motivates more students to participate due to the lowered associated costs of attendance, and to the shorter period of time away from their home countries. Academic agreements drawn up between the hosting schools and The College at Brockport permit students to take a broad range of liberal arts courses that may be applied to their degree program requirements back on campus upon their return, regardless of their academic majors and specific career interests.

The College at Brockport has sent as many as 500 students overseas to study abroad in an academic year. The current average participation is approximately 100 students in the fall and spring semesters, approximately 100-150 during the summer months and approximately 50 students over winter intersession. At present, Brockport has study abroad relationships with over 30 different Colleges and Universities in Antarctica, Australia, the Bahamas, China, Costa Rica, England, Estonia, Fiji, France, Ghana, Greece, India, Ireland, Italy, Jamaica, Kenya, Mexico, the Netherlands, New Zealand, the

Philippines, Poland, Romania, Russia, Scotland, Spain, Switzerland, Thailand and Vietnam.

## Student Acculturation

In terms of what we refer to as pastoral care – the care of the student both before and after actual travel occurs – The College at Brockport provides guidance to interested students in choosing the international program to attend. Each student is provided with pre-departure materials and each receives individual advising throughout their decision process. Students are required to apply to the programs, and our staff provides assistance with this process as well.

Students participate in an orientation program that is specific to the country and program to be entered. This sort of cultural acclimation is critical to the students' adaptation. Many of our programs include resident directors or program representatives who provide students with further assistance in the international location. These on-site representatives set up a range of programs and activities for students throughout the program study period. The College at Brockport also sends its own staff to partner colleges and universities as frequently as possible to maintain high quality standards in programming and to maintain good relationships with the hosting organizations with which we partner.

## Benefits to Students

There are countless personal benefits that flow to students who participate in study abroad experiences. They often become more sophisticated and more self-reflective; and improve their intellectual capacity and self-confidence. They enhance their resumes and add depth to their credentials, and in the process they become better prepared to enter an increasingly global work force. Students learn about their host country and its people, and they place both their prior education and their new studies in a different context that provides them with additional insights about their place in the world. Their new friends in host countries help them to create an invaluable network of international contacts. They learn about human values by personally integrating into another culture. Many improve their foreign language skills.

## Plans for the Future

In terms of the future, we intend to ramp up our international study abroad program offerings for both undergraduate and graduate students alike. Trends in study abroad programs are moving to shorter study tours of even less than a full semester in length and The College at Brockport has seen an increased amount of interest in such programs from both students and faculty members alike. The many advantages of offering study abroad programs to college students motivate us to continue to seek out additional academic partners, to create new study opportunities for graduate students, and to continue to benchmark our program against others with the aim of improving the experience for our students.

*Note: Susan Stites-Doe and Ralph Trecartin are, respectively, Dean of Graduate Studies and Executive Director of International Education at SUNY Brockport*

# V. GRADUATE INTERNATIONAL COLLABORATIONS AND THE FUTURE OF THE GLOBAL SCHOLARSHIP AND RESEARCH ENTERPRISE

## Summary of Presentations and Group Discussion

The fourth panel of the Global Summit widened the scope of earlier discussions, focusing on the evolving demands and opportunities of global scholarship and research. Panelists were invited to reflect on trends in academic and non-academic workforce demands in their national contexts as well as professional development resources designed to meet those demands. The panel was also a forum for considering what role graduate international collaborations might play in helping universities collect accurate data about the professional development needs of students and faculty and using that data to enhance international programs. The panel covered the following general questions:

- *The Thesis and Dissertation in a Cultural Context*: How is the dissertation viewed in different cultural or national contexts?
- *Career and Research Opportunities for Graduate Students and Future Scholars*: What research and career opportunities exist for students who have participated in global research and graduate education programs? What challenges do they face?
- *Development of Academic Staff and Faculty*: What opportunities and challenges exist for faculty conducting research within institutional partnerships?

Addressing the first question, **Austin McLean** (ProQuest) presented trends in the content, preservation, dissemination, and storage of theses and dissertations. As an electronic publisher, ProQuest has seen an increasing demand on the part of universities for electronic databases and indexes that increase the international accessibility of capstone projects. **Mr. McLean** asked summit participants to consider what principles might inform the creation of international electronic repositories of theses and dissertations in the current international research climate, a topic taken up again in the discussion.

Responding to the second and third questions, **Thomas Jørgensen** (European University Association) and **Karen DePauw** (Virginia Tech) delivered presentations on the preparation of faculty and graduate students for global research careers. **Dr. Jørgensen** reported on the drivers in the European context for encouraging the mobility of doctoral students—economic pressure for a mobile, European workforce and a stronger sense of European identity—and outlined the ways that graduate students and institutions are responding to this agenda. Recent EUA research[1] suggests that there is a greater need in Europe for doctorate-holders with "transferable skills" that go beyond discipline-specific research skills, and that students must also learn to recognize that they have acquired these skills and learn how to market them to future employers. European graduate institutions, in turn, must think critically about the transferable skills they aim to provide to graduate students through their programs. Speaking to the U.S. context, **Dr. DePauw** addressed the opportunities for faculty to pursue federal research grants for overseas research and the various ways that universities can support their professional preparation and development. For example, Virginia Tech provides coursework and other resources that equip faculty with skills training prior to their international experiences, such as language courses and pre-departure orientations that provide information on the material and cultural challenges they may encounter while conducting research in a different country.

During the discussion there was a strong emphasis on the need for universities and governments to provide more accurate maps of the current pathways between graduate programs and academic and non-academic careers. **Maxwell King** (Monash University) and **Debra Stewart** (CGS) reported that Australia and the U.S. lack substantial data on this question since the data are difficult to collect. **Dr. King** added that it is especially difficult to track students who enter non-academic careers, although in Australia, there is evidence that many of those who have pursued non-academic tracks are still engaged in some form of research. **Carolyn Watters** (Dalhousie University) proposed that in the absence of reliable data at the national level, institutions might consider engaging their own alumni networks in efforts to glean more information about the career pathways of students that have participated in international programs.

---

1   See EUA's DOC-CAREERS Project, Phase 1 (2006-08). The 2009 report, "Collaborative Doctoral Education": University-Industry Partnerships for Enhancing Knowledge Exchange, is available at http://www.eua.be/eua-work-and-policy-area/research-and-innovation/doctoral-education/doc-careers/

A related discussion topic was the need to examine further the challenges that graduate students and faculty confront as they leave academe for non-academic careers. **Dr. Jørgensen** noted that in Europe, the pipeline out of academe tends to operate in only one direction—it is nearly impossible to return to a university position after pursuing a non-academic career. **Allison Sekuler** (McMaster University) and **Dr. Watters** indicated that this was not the case in the Canadian context, where those who have pursued industry positions in science, engineering and business may have many opportunities to enter or reenter a university track. **Dr. Watters** added universities should consider providing support for returning professionals as they adjust to the new professional demands and cultural expectations that accompany a university position.

On the topic of repositories for theses and dissertations, summit participants shared a number of thoughts and ideas for improving the storing and dissemination of research. One set of observations concerned current debates about widening the range of languages that may be used in theses and dissertations. Some participants reported that as institutions question an older idea of dissertation databases—historically viewed as a record of national knowledge and memory—they must ensure that cultures and groups being studied have access to the information contained within such repositories. **Sheila Bonde** (Brown University) said that graduate students at Brown are trained about the ethical responsibility to publish in the language of the people being studied or included in the study group, and **Doug Peers** (York University) added that at his university, dissertations may be submitted in English, French, or any first nation's language in North America. This discussion suggests that the language of dissertation submission must be considered from an ethical and political perspective as well as a professional one.

Participants also discussed the use of new technologies to improve the quality and research value of international databases of research products. **Dick Strugnell** (University of Melbourne) said that digital dissertation repositories raise questions for many universities about the use of plagiarism software, and added that it would be helpful to create international best-practice principles that address this issue. **Dr. DePauw** observed that new technologies might also enhance the research process itself, not just its outcomes. She explained that resources such as electronic portfolios have the potential to document the outcomes of international research collaborations as well as the important "process of getting there." Panel Chair **Lesley Wilson** (EUA) suggested that these topics, as well as the relationship between national and international dissertation repositories, be further considered in summit dialogues about the role of technology in supporting graduate education and research.

While panel four covered a broad range of issues surrounding the relationship between graduate international collaborations and the global research enterprise, the discussion suggested that a topic of particular importance and urgency was the professional development of graduate students. Ultimately, international, national and institutional research about workforce needs will need to examine this question closely, and the answers to the question will need to inform the content and support systems surrounding university-to-university partnerships.

# Preservation and Discovery of Theses and Dissertations: An International Perspective

Austin McLean
ProQuest

Jim McGinty
Cambridge Information Group

## Introduction

ProQuest supports the goals of graduate education by disseminating research to national and international audiences. The purpose of this paper is to share our observations relating to the publication of Ph.D. and Master's theses, and provide our perspective on confronting the array of change that has affected Ph.D. and Master's theses over the past several years. These observations have been garnered from our experience publishing Ph.D. and Master's theses for 1,700 graduate institutions over the past 70 years, and disseminating over 2.7 million theses, a total of more than 80,000 new works each year.

We identify two catalysts driving change in the dissertation world. The first is the shifting of Ph.D. and Master's theses from analog formats (microfilm and paper) to electronic formats (digital). The second is the emergence of new software technologies, which has enabled search and discovery of scholarly works throughout the international research community. Five trends have emerged:

**(1) Dissemination and Discovery:** The overarching element driving the migration of the graduate thesis from paper to electronic format has been the rise of the internet. Researchers have a desire to participate in this worldwide knowledge exchange, both by ensuring that their research is discovered, and working to make certain that they are aware of the latest trends in their field. Clearly, universities and authors have a strong incentive to ensure the widest dissemination and discovery of their scholarly output. Web publishing has become a key dissemination strategy for most universities. However, simply placing theses on a website does not ensure their visibility worldwide. More and more universities are turning to publishers with the expertise and infrastructure to provide added value, via tagging and editorial expertise, in the web dissemination process. Publishers have time-tested vehicles in the form of databases and indexes to deliver content to researchers, who are pressed for time and want a precise searching mechanism that guarantees the return of relevant results. By placing graduate works in the path of researchers via published databases and indexes, universities believe they are maximizing the accessibility of their materials to a worldwide audience.

**(2) Preservation:** The notion that university-sponsored, graduate-level research must be preserved and maintained has been with us for a long time. Preserving research is fraught with challenges, and for decades universities have been partnering with the private sector to leverage best practices. Currently there is a sea change occurring as preservation moves from an analog, paper and microfilm-based strategy to a digital, electronic file-based system. The standards for digital preservation continue to evolve and change, but we have seen a number of key trends emerging. Ensuring the integrity and authenticity of files via frequent data checks is once such development. Digital preservation is proven to be more costly than analog preservation, and many observers are concerned about budget ramifications of digital preservation. This is leading to cooperative projects among institutions. As with analog preservation, many universities are working with companies like ProQuest to help offset the cost of digital preservation.

**(3) Translation:** Translation of theses is a significant issue in the worldwide graduate research community. In our experience, supplying an abstract in more than one language is an effective strategy for broadening research dissemination. The editorial recommendation for the ProQuest Dissertations and Theses Database is that a citation be provided in the native language of the country where the work is created, along with a version of the abstract in English. While this may not be surprising given that ProQuest is based in an English-speaking country, similar recommendations have been found in other countries, such as China, which has a requirement that all theses contain a citation and abstract in both Chinese and English. The 80,000 authors who annually publish their theses using Proquest are advised to consult their advisors or department chairpersons for guidance about translation, since advisors are in the best position to explain disciplinary conventions related to multilingual requirements.

**(4) Institutional Repositories:** Over the past 10 years the establishment of institutional repositories, websites that strive to host the entirety of a university's research output, has become a growing trend. The notion of a central location for an entire university's research output has been positively received by many in the library community. However, many libraries have started institutional repositories only to meet resistance on the part of faculty and/or graduate students. This is due in part to the academic reward system, which is more focused on publishing articles in prestigious journals than in ensuring that content resides in a centralized institutional location. As a method for driving author participation, funding agencies and universities have begun to mandate the placement of publicly funded research in repositories. Ph.D. and Master's theses are frequently targeted for inclusion in university repositories. ProQuest receives frequent questions about the role of repositories in relation to our own Dissertation and Master's Theses Database, and we have worked to ensure that these repositories complement one another. Maximizing the number of locations where the research can be made available is a tactic adopted by researchers and universities aiming to put theses in the path of researchers. In 2008 alone, the ProQuest Dissertation and Theses database had over 180 million searches from thousands of researchers in more than 3,000 libraries. Many university repositories are also reporting heavy usage.

**(5) Multimedia Content:** Along with the change in format of theses from paper to electronic, the nature and scope of graduate work has changed as well. Our experience is that many theses have a significant complement of non page-based material such as audio or video material, data sets, executables or other digital material. Typically this content is supplemental to the page-based material, providing the graduate committee with additional data related to the student's work. Occasionally ProQuest encounters culminating projects consisting entirely of multimedia content, especially when the thesis is in the area of communications or theater. (Although the admissibility of this content varies by institution, some institutions have accepted this content for some time. ProQuest received its first all digital Ph.D. thesis more than a decade ago). In some cases, university regulations limit the use of multimedia content; for example, universities in North America continue to require that only page-based material be included in completed Ph.D. and Master's theses. While the acceptance of multimedia content first arose at technology-focused universities, this practice has since spread to some departments at other types of top-tier universities. Over the next three years, we expect a significant increase in the number of universities that not only allow multimedia theses, but also actively promote this format among students. Within seven years we expect near universal acceptance of multimedia theses among North American universities.

## Conclusion/Next Steps

It is apparent to us that the world of scholarly communications is changing rapidly, and we believe that it is important to be aware of the range of issues shaping the preservation of theses and dissertations in various regions and countries. To this end we look forward to further discussion of questions shaping this segment of the panel, in particular:

1. Given the current climate of international research, what principles might inform the creation of international electronic repositories of theses and dissertations?

2. Given that many countries still maintain national repositories of theses and dissertations, what principles would best support a complementary relationship between national and international databases?

# Mobility, Skills and Careers

## Thomas Ekman Jørgensen
## European University Association

The theme of international mobility and the labour market has been on the European agenda for a long time. It has been an important topic for the very ambitious Lisbon Strategy set out a decade ago to make the EU the most dynamic and competitive knowledge-based economy in the world. From the point of view of political stakeholders, increased international mobility would create a more flexible labour force that in turn would overcome the perceived problems of fragmented labour markets within the European Union, realising the free movement of persons that is a basic principle of the European Internal Market.

Concerning higher education, the Bologna Process has aimed at introducing comparable structures to facilitate recognition and make the learning trajectory of individual students more transparent. In terms of funding, the Erasmus Programme of the European Union has become a broadly recognised programme with about 160,000 students at the undergraduate and Master's level participating in 2006/2007. For the doctoral level, the Marie Curie programme of the EU has a budget of approximately 1.9 billion Euros allocated to "Initial Training Networks" for 2007-2013, facilitating mobility in doctoral education through joint programmes. Although this is mostly aiming at internal European mobility, the participants certainly feel that they are exposed to an international experience in a foreign cultural setting. Even going the relatively short distance from Vienna in Austria to Budapest in Hungary or Bologna in Italy will require a fair deal of cultural and academic adjustment and in turn the flexibility and cultural openness that are among the main goals of the mobility experience.

On the global scale, Europe is a growing net importer of students with the UK a key player in the global higher education arena as well as Germany and France. The Bologna Process has increased awareness about the European Higher Education Area and initiatives such as the Erasmus Mundus Programme are a very visible part of the many global co-operations; this development gives some European campuses a truly international atmosphere and creates possibilities to integrate intercultural dialogue within the university wall, or to practise "internationalisation at home."

These developments towards increased international mobility has, particularly for doctoral education, been mirrored (although to a lesser extent) by initiatives for inter-sectoral mobility. Structures have been set up on the national level such as the industrial PhD (particularly in the Nordic Countries) or the French CIFRE programme, where the research project of the doctoral candidate is carried out at or in close co-operation with a private company. Funded by the research council, Vitae in the UK is an example of an organisation that works as a platform for dialogue about research careers for all the relevant stakeholders. However, the structures to support intersectoral mobility and research careers are very diverse in different countries.

International and inter-sectoral mobility meet in the discussion about transferable skills, skills that are not connected to a specific discipline or career path. The skills discussion has been high on the agenda for some years and is still developing as a main means to break down cultural barriers between different sectors. Talking about skills in terms of generic abilities such as flexibility, creative thinking or management skills is seen as a way of communicating the qualities of researchers beyond the narrow, discipline-oriented technical competencies and knowledge. In this vein, the Irish Universities have published a common *Ph.D. Graduates' Skills*; the aforementioned Vitae (the UK GRAD) similarly issued a skills statement (*Joint Statement of the UK Research Councils' Training Requirements for Research Students*) which is to be expanded and revised in the immediate future.

In the context of international mobility, the skills (in the broadest sense of the word) acquired would, among others, include mental openness and flexibility, improved social skills, intercultural communication and—more tangibly—language skills.

The European University Association (EUA) has contributed considerably to the issue of skills. In 2005, the provision of skills training was one of the Salzburg Principles that has since been the basis of the reforms of doctoral education in Europe, and the EUA reports doctoral programmes (*Doctoral Programmes for the European Knowledge Society* from 2005 and *Doctoral Programmes in Europe's Universities: Achievements and Challenges* from 2007) dealt at length with the issue of skills provision in doctoral programmes. From 2006 to 2008, the EUA DOC-CAREERS project produced evidence about university-industry collaboration with considerable weight on the skills issue (collected in the report *Collaborative Doctoral Education 2009*). One important finding of this project was that the transferable skills requested particularly by large companies were the ones that connected social and communication skills, management, creative thinking, capacity to deal with complex, multidisciplinary work and team work. These are very much the skills that are supposedly acquired through experiences of international mobility. Intra-sectoral mobility between universities in different countries thus furthers inter-sectoral mobility both directly and indirectly by enhancing the qualities that are requested of researchers in the private sector. In fact, the EUA study explicitly shows how lack of international experiences can be a reason to turn down otherwise well-qualified candidates.

The central point of the whole discussion about skills is very much about awareness. Only a limited spectrum of skills can be directly taught; others are skills acquired through the research experience, including mobility experiences. It is hence essential for doctoral programmes to find ways to enhance the awareness of acquired skills in addition to providing direct training. Doctorate holders who are aware of their skills and are able to communicate them will generally have better and more diverse career opportunities.

The academic labour market in Europe is still rather fragmented. Entering an academic position from the outside of a national academic community can be difficult (obviously more for some disciplines than others—law would be an extreme example of a very national discipline); even finding academic job advertisements require country-specific knowledge as only a limited number of positions are advertised at the European level. The basic structures of a European academic labour market are only being constructed. The European Commission's Euraxess portal is for example an attempt to create common European job advertisements, but is still not widely used. Traditionally, staying close to the local research environment has been one of the most efficient strategies for finding employment in the academic sector. However, universities are articulating more precise strategies and constructing stronger profiles. At the same time, enhanced focus on autonomy, quality assurance and accountability means that recruitment policies are getting more transparent and aim at enhancing the individual institutional profile. In such a situation, applicants that can prove their international network and demonstrate a varied career path will have a head start compared to those that before had a "home advantage." The wish of many universities to enhance their international profile as well as the weight of international publications in the various rankings could increase the chances of those with an international experience even further. There is also a good chance that the transferable skills of an applicant with an international experience, such as flexibility, language skills or social skills, will be easier to demonstrate for those that have received their doctorate from a programme with a visible, even certified, international element.

Institutional strategies to further awareness and not least communication and attestation of the transferable skills linked to international mobility certainly include formal co-operations such as joint programmes with specific joint degrees. Others combine mobility with organised inter-cultural experiences on-campus. This can be through summer schools with partner universities giving a short, intensive exposure to an international environment or transferable skills training that teach or bring awareness about inter-cultural communication.

Having a degree from a joint programme is a way to make the mobility experience visible to potential employers. Some European doctoral programmes set up their joint programmes according to the European Doctorate or *Doctor Europeus* that has a standardised set of criteria for the international (European) element of the programme. Other programmes have specific joint or dual degrees that demonstrate the doctorate holder's international experience. However, some institutions find that the cumbersome process of setting up joint programmes, while worthwhile for the larger, cohort-based Master's programmes, do not serve doctoral programmes very well. Doctoral candidates have much more individual needs and unique trajectories that call for more flexible and individually tailored mobility options. These universities deal with the problem of communicating mobility experiences through a "doctoral certificate" or diploma supplement where the institution attests the participation in a range of possible international activities without necessarily having a special joint or dual degree. In this way, the specific mobility experience of the doctorate holder is certified by the university for future employers.

This report demonstrates the very diverse strategies that universities employ to create possibilities for international experiences, enhance the awareness about the skills acquired through the experiences and certify this experience when conveying doctorates.

# *Development of Academic Staff and Faculty*

## Karen P. DePauw
## Virginia Tech

Academic personnel comprise a valuable resource and are critical to building and sustaining successful international graduate collaborations. Key among these are the individuals known as faculty in the U.S. and, in the European context, "academic staff," who provide quality graduate education and research experiences for graduate students. Although highly educated and prepared as scholars and teachers in higher education settings within their country, faculty (academic staff) haven't always had access to or taken advantage of programs and opportunities to enhance their working knowledge and skill sets for participating in international graduate education collaborations. Further, as global scholarship is important to the research enterprise and graduate education, faculty could also take advantage of opportunities that exist to expand their research endeavors and those of their graduate students.

Academic staff (faculty) often have an established network for collaboration in research and scholarship with colleagues within the same university, at different universities or with researchers outside higher education. With increasing technology and its availability worldwide, individual faculty members have expanded their networks to include international collaborators and global partners. To assist in the process of expanding networks and collaborators, faculty could take advantage of the individualized opportunities and highly regarded existing programs. Perhaps the most notable of these is the Fulbright Scholar Program available within the United States and around the world. In addition to the Fulbright program, discipline-based and interdisciplinary international fellowship programs are available at the national U.S. level (e.g., ASEE International Fellowships, Ford Fellowships, Asia Institute Fellowships, SSRC fellowships). Fellowships are available for faculty from many countries and regions worldwide. Two examples include fellowships from the Swiss National Science Foundation and fellowship from ERICM (European Research Consortium on Informatics and Mathematics) for Ph.D. holders worldwide. These are many others are available through GrantsNet: International Funding Index hosted by *Science*.

Opportunities might also exist within one's university. These are often identified as research leaves, sabbaticals, faculty research exchanges, faculty fellowships, and international faculty development programs. Research leaves, sabbaticals and fellowships have been offered by most U.S. universities and are available for international experiences. A recent development is the offering of international faculty development programs which include short-term visits by an interdisciplinary team of faculty to partner universities to explore potential research collaboration and possible graduate degree collaborations (e.g., Virginia Tech International Faculty Development Program (IFDP)). Once the initial contact is made through the sabbatical, fellowships or IFDP, a partnership can be developed with faculty visits, short term exchanges for faculty and graduate students, long-term research collaboration, and even job opportunities for faculty, graduate students and postdocs.

Professional development needs vary in accordance with the type and goals of the international collaborations but essentially, all academic staff (faculty) should have a basic level of cultural awareness and understanding that increases with their involvement with international collaborations. University organized pre-departure orientations assist faculty in understanding issues related to short-term visits and extended professional travel and specific requirements when students are participating (e.g., health insurance, vaccinations, evacuation requirements, orientation to the country, housing logistics, money, student policies, visa requirements, passport, government travel warnings and restrictions). University-organized foreign language instruction programs designed specifically for faculty and staff exist, and they can be helpful in preparing for international collaborative efforts.

The experience of faculty conducting research within institutional partnerships can be enhanced through attention to a number of issues articulated below. These include the following:

- Understanding partner institutions from different cultural perspectives
- Understanding the differences in university organization and structures including the different types of universities, university funding, academic units and departments, and research enterprise and corporate relations, etc.
- Understanding differences in terminology – different words for similar concepts and same words with different meanings such as faculty/college, faculty/academic staff, training/education, and more
- Establishing a level of cultural competence for the country or region of destination including foreign language competence and ability to communicate effectively
- Understanding different academic cultures and practices throughout the world including topics such as:
  o Definitions of academic staff or faculty; graduate students or

postgraduate student (doctoral)
- o Publications – writing style, authorship, journals
- o Intellectual property, copyright and fair use concerns, patents, trademarks
- o Ethics and professional standards and Responsible Conduct of Research
- o Academic degrees requirements, admissions, courses, grades, examinations, etc.
- o The faculty-student relationship and different mentoring approaches
- o Policies and procedures
- • Securing human and financial resources to support global research and scholarship; the time needed to prepare for and engage in global scholarship

Faculty development is a key component of any academic endeavor, but especially for global collaborations. Many offices are available within Virginia Tech to assist with these efforts and they are more than willing to help faculty realize a high-quality global experience and those of their graduate students and colleagues as well.

# VI. NEW GLOBAL NETWORKS OF OPPORTUNITY AND SUPPORT

## Summary of Presentations and Group Discussion

In the opening panel, presenters stressed that both universities and governments have a vested interest in coordinating their efforts to internationalize graduate institutions at both the national and international levels. The final panel of the Global Summit returned to this topic, focusing on the growing number of national and global networks that are working to construct common or complementary priorities for collaborative research and education. Panel five was also designed to stimulate thinking about potential networks that might be developed to address the many challenges that remain in this area. Four sets of questions framed the papers and discussion:

- *International Collaborations and Capacity-Building*: What opportunities and challenges exist for graduate international collaborations between countries with unequal resources?
- *The Role of National and International Organizations*: What opportunities exist for building new networks of collaboration and support? What role might national and international organizations play in building and supporting such networks?
- *Best Practice Research and Outcomes Assessment*: What principles guide the creation and maintenance of successful programs, and how can their success and/or outcomes be measured?
- *Model Programs*: What strong models exist for future graduate international collaborations? What lessons have been learned in the process of creating them?

As was stressed in earlier panels, the most pressing global problems in health, environment, and agriculture are most deeply felt in developing countries, and there have been increasing efforts on the part of governments and universities to build collaborative networks and partnerships that seek to build capacity in these areas. **Allison Sekuler** (McMaster University) and **Helene Marsh** (James Cook University) examined some of the myths and realities surrounding these types of collaborations—partnerships that are too often considered "missionary" programs from the perspective of wealthier countries and universities. **Dr. Sekuler** noted that in effect, most collaborations are neither "missionary" nor "mercenary" but some combination of the two forms. If one thinks of capacity-building as philanthropic, she added, there is also the risk of overlooking the non-material benefits that often accrue to the wealthier partner (recruitment of talented students, enhanced research capacities, and the ability to work on problems with strong global impact), as well as the fact that countries in the course of development may become lateral partners later on. **Dr. Marsh** gave close attention to the processes by which first-world countries can truly follow through on the goal of "building capacity": encouraging students from developing countries to pursue topics of interest to their home countries and equipping them to independently pursue research funding after graduation are two key strategies for helping students to capitalize on their educational experiences.

The issue of capacity-building was also taken up in the next set of presentations on the current and potential role of national and international organizations in supporting research collaborations. Both **John Hayton** (Australian Education International) and **Carolyn Watters** (Dalhousie University) stressed the need to include a larger number of countries in strategic discussions of international collaborations, including the Global Summit. **Mr. Hayton** added that the shift from national to global governance through forums such as the G-20 may be an important opportunity for recognizing the value of international research and education for all countries. **Dr. Watters** seconded this point and added that there needs to be increased dialogue between universities, government sectors supporting economic development, funding agencies, NGO's and corporations about the role of graduate education in supporting the international economy and addressing pressing social and environmental problems.

Next, **Lesley Wilson** (European University Association) and **Daniel Denecke** (CGS) discussed the role of national and regional university associations in collecting data about graduate international collaborations and disseminating best practice in this area. **Ms. Wilson** reported that following the successive waves of Europeanization and internationalization, European universities through their associations and with other stakeholders have developed common standards that provide a framework for collaborations between different types of universities in different national contexts: these include standards and guidelines for external quality assurance and tool-kits that help to promote mobility and the recognition of study abroad periods. Addressing the U.S. context, **Dr. Denecke** outlined a number of the key outcomes of CGS' NSF-funded Graduate International Collaborations Project, which examined the challenges of developing graduate international collaborations, including joint and dual degree programs, and promising practices for building and sustaining international partnerships. One of the most important conclusions of the CGS study is that there is a need for more coordinated efforts to assess the outcomes of international collaborations for local economies, institutions, faculty, and graduate students. Such assessment could help universities demonstrate to state and local governments the concrete outcomes of their investments in international collaborations.

The final presentation was given by **Maxwell King** (Monash University), who used a case study to demonstrate the process by which his institution developed strong institutional ties with Indian Institute of Technology in Bombay through the development of an international joint degree program. **Dr. King** emphasized one of the points that had been stressed in the discussions following panel three, the importance of proceeding with a collaboration through gradual process steps. He also noted that it is important for universities to be aware that collaborations go through different stages of development and to address key concerns, like educational programming for graduate students, before focusing on research capacity within the program.

During the discussion period participants examined some of the greatest challenges that universities and governments face as they work toward better harmonization of policies and practices surrounding graduate international collaboration. A key concern was the tension between university and government agendas for internationalization and the need for better coordination between them. **Dr. Sekuler** pointed out that there need to be special efforts to coordinate university priorities with those of state and provincial governments. For example, universities many find that collaborations and the foreign students they help recruit will have important social and economic benefits, even if international visitors do not remain in Canada, whereas the perception on the part of provincial governments may be different. Speaking at a larger national and regional level, **Jean Chambaz** (Université Pierre et Marie Curie) and **Ms. Wilson** noted that national governments need input from universities in order to make informed decisions about international higher education policy. **Dr. Chambaz** added that university-government coordination can be most successful when university leaders take the initiative to define priorities. He noted that the 2005 Salzburg seminar on "Doctoral Programmes for the European Knowledge Economy" was an example of a successful effort to participate in the shaping of international higher education policy, since the principles recommended by the seminar participants[1] were later endorsed by the European Union's Council of Ministers.

Participants also discussed a number of ideas and strategies for broadening and organizing the discussion of graduate international collaborations. Many noted that one of the greatest challenges of organizing the ongoing discussion is that it concerns so many different groups and sectors within academe, government, industry, and a broad range of countries with different priorities. **Dr. Chambaz** recommended that the solution is not to include all of these groups around the same table but to create many different dialogues among stakeholders with common concerns and interests. Additional groups listed for inclusion were accrediting bodies, which often have a direct effect on the ways that universities develop collaborations; international groups and agencies involved in the regulation of research and the development of policies for research ethics in the context of international collaborations; and groups that support postdoctoral training and research.

Throughout the discussion of government and university coordination efforts, participants emphasized the need for empirical measurements that demonstrate the impact of graduate international collaborations on graduate students and universities. **Dr. Sekuler** specifically mentioned a need for metrics that illustrate the career pathways of international students: "When students come to your country, learn about your culture, repatriate and then give you these channels and networks, there are tremendous benefits, but that is a hard story to tell [without metrics]." **Jeffery Gibeling** (University of California, Davis) added that it would be useful to measure the extent to which joint or dual degree programs affect a student's academic socialization: "We know that academic socialization is a key aspect of graduate student success, so academic socialization presumably will foster greater academic research success; however, this needs to be measured." Participants agreed that given the more widespread trend toward quality assessment and accountability measurement in graduate education, such metrics will not only be useful, but necessary.

---

1    For more information about the Salzburg Principles, see the EUA website at http://www.eua.be/research/doctoral-programmes/doctoral-programmes-in-the-bologna-process/salzburg-seminar/

ALLISON B. SEKULER

# International Collaboration and Capacity-Building: Creating "Davincis-By-Committee"

## Allison B. Sekuler
## McMaster University

*The futures we inherit are not of our own making, but the futures we create for generations of young people who follow us arise out of our ability to imagine a better world, recognize our responsibility to others, and define the success of a society to the degree that it can address the needs of coming generations to live in a world in which the obligations of a global democracy and individual responsibility mutually inform each other.*

–Henry A. Giroux, from "Translating the future and the promise of democracy," convocation address, Memorial University, 2005.

I recently sat on a panel tasked with answering the question: Will there ever be another daVinci? The consensus of our group - an artist, an engineer, and a neuroscientist – was, "No." Since the time of daVinci, research has become increasingly specialized, funding has become more linked to short-term economic gains, and the most critical questions have become more global. Our view was that there might not be another daVinci, but there certainly could be a daVinci-by-committee: a group of people who might come together to solve the world's big problems, combining a range of backgrounds and skill sets to create something much greater than the sum of its parts.

Key to the idea of daVinci-by-committee is the notion of international collaboration and capacity building. Will the crucial member of daVinci-by-committee be from the United States? Canada? Argentina? China? Ghana? The unique life experiences of each person shape the way problems are identified and solved, and individuals from different backgrounds bring dramatically different abilities and perspectives to the table.

In my own field of neuroscience, we have seen evidence that even something as basic as face recognition is influenced by one's cultural background—observers from Canada rely much more on the region around the eyes for face recognition than do observers from Japan. Similar cultural effects are seen in comparisons of Western versus Eastern scene processing. If these fundamental perceptual processes are influenced by culture, imagine the

*Global Perspectives on Graduate International Collaborations*     **113**

effect of culture on our perception of the environment, clean water, infectious disease, and green energy.

By increasing international graduate collaborations, we can provide new perspectives to old problems, develop broader capacity, and address issues that could not otherwise be addressed. Of course, there are other benefits to these collaborations as well: universities can enhance their reputations, increase cultural awareness, form valuable new research alliances, and sometimes make a profit along the way. Through international collaborations we can create and drive new policies and markets, increase diversity (including increased opportunities for women in science), provide role models for our under-represented students, and address issues of accessibility, particularly when universities in high-income countries (HIC) partner with those in low- and middle-income countries (LMIC).

The issue of accessibility certainly is not new. In his report to President Truman on the post-war future of science, Vannevar Bush noted: "There are talented individuals in every segment of the population, but with few exceptions those without the means of buying higher education go without it. Here is a tremendous waste of the greatest resource of a nation—the intelligence of its citizens. ("Science—the endless frontier," July, 1945). Bush's comments specifically concerned science education and development in the United States, but the same sentiment holds true for all areas of scholarship, worldwide, and international collaborations yield synergistic advantages. HIC universities can provide unimaginable resources and learning opportunities for students (and faculty) from LMIC universities; and students (and faculty) from LMIC universities can provide unimaginable talent and unique perspectives to HIC universities.

McMaster University has a long history of international collaborations and capacity building, particularly in the areas of nursing and the life and health sciences. For example, McMaster faculty worked with the Aga Khan University (AKU) to support the development of academic programs in nursing in Pakistan. Since that first collaboration in 1979, the joint program of developing professional training and leadership opportunities for women and improving healthcare has spread to numerous other countries, including Kenya, Tanzania, Uganda, Afghanistan, Syria and Egypt. Twenty-three years later, in renewing and expanding the collaboration between McMaster and AKU, His Highness the Aga Khan noted that "when governments are fragile, it is civil society which comes in and sustains the development process. Professional nursing, educating women, is an absolutely fundamental pillar to the building of society."

McMaster faculty recognize that one's education should not be limited by the accident of one's birthplace. Faculty in Biology at McMaster worked with colleagues in Jamaica to set up an aquatic ecology lab at the University of the West Indies (UWI), leading not only to enhanced learning opportunities for students at UWI, but also increased opportunities for Canadian researchers in a unique environmental setting and increased connections to UWI's Centre for Marine Sciences. UWI and McMaster University also partnered in developing a stand-alone oncology nursing program in Trinidad.

On a larger scale, long before it became vogue to develop international branch campuses for North American universities, McMaster faculty understood that they had a responsibility to ensure that high quality education was accessible in all corners of the world. In 2001, the first class graduated from the College of Health Sciences at the University of Sharjah, developed through an extensive collaboration in which McMaster faculty "trained the trainers" and worked with faculty and staff at the University of Sharjah to develop high quality health science programs, adapted from McMaster's own successful approach to clinical training. Although the intent of these partnerships was for capacity building, not personal or institutional gain, the collaborations led to even stronger relationships, recently culminating in the generous donation of an endowed Chair in Global Islam to McMaster University from His Highness Sheikh Dr. Sultan Bin Mohammed Al-Qasimi, Ruler of Sharjah.

Of course, challenges exist in these asymmetric partnerships. There are differential levels of facilities and communication infrastructure; political, cultural, and linguistic differences; differences in the strategic priorities of institutions and nations; differences in the culture and laws surrounding intellectual property, technology transfer, academic freedom, and ownership of ideas; and differences in the degree of specialization and accessibility to diverse educational opportunities. Critically, HIC and LMIC institutions often have different levels of access to investment from the government, the public sector, and the private sector. And when funding is available, it may be overly dispersed, diluted, hyper-specialized (both geographically and topically), and driven by short-term outcomes. To succeed in building international collaborations, we need increased coordination of funding opportunities, and long-term commitments.

Fortunately, governments, the public sector, and the private sector are increasingly realizing the importance on international, and often interdisciplinary, collaborations to address today's big problems. Government agencies, such as Canada's Social Sciences and Humanities Research Council (SSHRC), Natural Sciences and Engineering Research Council (NSERC), and the Canadian Institutes for Health Research (CIHR), have begun setting aside specific pools of funding to encourage international collaboration, and consortia of international agencies have begun to form to provide increased coordination in support of international collaboration and capacity building. Private organizations, such as the Human Frontier Science Program, have programs specifically geared at developing international collaborations, and repatriating researchers after their international stays. The private sector also increasingly sees value in supporting international collaborations. All of these funds, however, remain a relatively small proportion of overall budgets, and not all of the funds may be directly applicable to support of graduate student initiatives.

Fortunately, the costs of international collaboration can be minimized, while increasing the number and range of collaborations, by taking advantage of new technologies. Although nothing can replace the value of a truly immersive, person-to-person international experience, those experiences can be augmented by virtual communications. The addition of virtual experiences to international collaborations can go a long way toward ensuring critical mass in programs, and to facilitate follow-up communications after on-site experiences. Although high-level video conferencing centres may not be available in all regions, access to communications networks is increasing rapidly around the world – indeed, a recent report from the United Nations University Institute for Water, Environment and Health notes that people in some regions around the world now have more access to cell phones than they do to adequate sanitation. The increased communications infrastructure and access provides a relatively inexpensive way to establish and maintain international collaborations (although, obviously, many parts of the world, particularly in LMICs, remain un-linked). For example, McMaster University recently developed several globally-focused graduate programs in which on-site international research experience is complemented by on-line international interactions. Open campuses at institutions like UWI are also making education accessible to a wider range of individuals, and the development of infrastructure related to those open campuses provide great opportunity to build international collaborations. And, as HIC universities increasingly expand with "branch campuses" in LMICs, they, by necessity, bring with them infrastructure that can support improved distance learning. One can also take advantage of communications infrastructure of national and international organizations outside the traditional university environment, at NGOs and other public and private organizations.

Of course, the nature of what is being taught through international collaborations will necessarily differ from traditional intra-national courses. It is critical to understand that the benefits and outcomes for learners from different cultures may differ considerably. This fact needs to be taken into account as we develop appropriate methods to address issues of assessment and accountability (e.g., an issue of increasing concern for organizations that support international collaborations, such as the HFSP, IRDC, and OECD). Most importantly, we need to ensure that the skills we are teaching are transferable to other environments. In that sense, the focus on 21$^{st}$ century skills is particularly important in international programs. Problem solving, synthesis, communication, networking, adapting: these skills, in addition to standard disciplinary content, will ensure that students can make the most of their education in any environment, and that they understand the extent to which all environments are increasingly interconnected. With these skills students from any part of the world can bring their ingenuity and insights to a daVinci-by-Committee.

> . . . *the more globalised and interdependent the world becomes, the more we need great collaborators and orchestrators, not isolated individuals, no matter how well they do.*
> Angel Gurrîa, OECD Secretary-General, UNESCO, Paris, France, October, 2009

# *International Collaboration and Capacity-Building: Promising Policies and Practices for a Global Knowledge Society*

**Helene Marsh**
**James Cook University**

**Barbara Evans**
**University of British Columbia**

**Barbara Kehm**
**University of Kassel**

**Margaret Kiley**
**Australian National University**

**Rachel Pitt**
**University of Queensland**

**Andrea Stith**
**Shanghai Jiao Tong University**

The increasing importance of innovation for the knowledge society is widely acknowledged as is the central role that highly trained researchers play in society. The quality of training provided to researchers through the doctoral and postdoctoral periods, their mobility, and the mobility of their intellectual capital are important influences on the innovation capabilities of institutions, regions, countries, and global networks.

For many decades, support for academic mobility has been a major tool of international cooperation with the aim of strengthening research and advanced training capacities in less developed countries. Such mobility has been seen as a key mechanism for jump-starting modern science and advanced training in the colonial and post-colonial world and a priority for official development assistance programs, intergovernmental agencies, and international philanthropic organisations. Governments in less developed countries take advantage of such international assistance to invest heavily in overseas training to strengthen domestic capacity in science and higher education. Nonetheless, at the same time such capacity is constantly eroded by the recruitment of scientists and scholars from developing countries to more attractive positions in the developed world and the tendency for international students to seek temporary or permanent migration status upon graduation.

Access to talented doctoral candidates who are able to contribute financially to universities and higher education systems by undertaking research and/or paying fees has also been an important goal for more developed countries. The desire to maximize the social and economic benefits garnered from cutting-edge science and technology drives many nations to develop innovation strategies, with the resulting income being seen as "big business" for many systems and institutions.

Policy-makers are increasingly seeking strategic advantage by building and capitalizing on talent. Increasingly, the short-term migration of PhD holders across national borders is seen as a sensible means of boosting a nation's skill or knowledge base. Thus, policies increasingly focus on building national research capacity by shaping the demographic of highly-trained PhD researchers to assume a global leadership position in science and technology. While the host countries benefit such policies may have a detrimental impact on the sending countries by depleting their highly trained talent, despite many doctoral graduates maintaining financial, cultural and political links with their home country.

Increasingly, individuals keen to experience alternative education systems have been motivated to undertake research development outside their home environment to provide international and cross-cultural perspectives for learner researchers. This aim can be motivated by a sending country, whether developed or developing, an institution, a discipline, and/or an individual. Researchers, particularly in the sciences, have long realized the benefits and desirability of academic exchange, but this practice has been expanded and embraced enthusiastically by other fields as well.

Competition for talent between nations has strengthened as the number of highly-trained researchers has increased. The percentage of international students enrolled in advanced research programs (including doctoral programs) in various countries is not uniform. For example, only 15.7 percent of international students in the United States are enrolled in advanced research programs. For other counties, the percentage is even less (United Kingdom 11.6 percent, France and Japan each 10.1 percent, Canada 9.8 percent, Australia 4.2 percent).

Many policies are designed to facilitate the mobility of doctoral candidates: short-term exchanges (two years or less), the development of processes for recognition of international degrees, the convergence of programs of doctoral education across national boundaries, the establishment of overseas campuses by tertiary education institutions, the development of joint/shared programs, and the increasing emphasis on the English language.

Research on undergraduate students suggests that the presence of international doctoral candidates on campus will not automatically lead to greater intercultural understanding and awareness by either international or domestic doctoral candidates, a view supported by anecdotal evidence from international student officers on various campuses. Pro-active institutional intervention is required to develop effective communication and collaboration between international and domestic candidates as equal partners in the doctoral learning experience.

The topic is complicated by different opinions about the value of the pre-eminence of English as a common language in doctoral programs. Some scholars criticize the dominance of English, deploring the consequential loss of capacity to research topics that are language-specific. Others argue that the widespread use of English provides an effective tool to facilitate and enhance the cross-cultural dialogue between domestic and international students, especially in their research and doctoral education activities.

In the apparent absence of studies specific to trainee researchers, we suggest several possible interventions below which institutions might try, preferably as part of a controlled study to provide an evidence base to inform future initiatives. These policies are summarized in Box 1 below.

**Box 1: Promising practices for doctoral and postdoctoral education for a global knowledge society.**

---

**Recruitment:**
- Select candidates in collaboration with home country institutions, with mutual mentoring.
- Encourage faculty to develop research collaborations with researchers in potential sending countries as basis for developing joint doctoral degree programs.
- Encourage international candidates to enroll in a joint degree with a university in their sending country.
- Encourage international doctoral and postdoctoral candidates to pursue topics of importance and interest to their sending country.

---

**During candidature and the postdoctoral period in a receiving country:**

- Provide assistance in meeting the personal and logistical challenges of settling into the receiving country.
- Provide orientation programs to help doctoral candidates and post-docs understand the personal and professional norms of the receiving country.
- Assist candidates/postdoctoral appointees in understanding the expectations of their doctoral or postdoctoral program.
- Train faculty and student leaders committed to the internationalization of research training.
- Train faculty to work effectively in cross-cultural situations including classroom and research group settings to maximize the mutual learning between domestic and international students/postdoctoral appointees.
- Provide specialist language support in the context of the research program.
- Introduce peer-pairing programs between domestic and international candidates/postdoctoral appointees.
- Assist candidates/postdoctoral appointees to develop links with government, academia, and industry in the sending country via conferences, publications (including in the candidates' native language), presentations, teaching, and collaborative research.
- Provide training in writing grant applications.
- Provide literature access and professional support throughout the training period a in both the sending and receiving countries.

**At the end of candidature/postdoctoral appointment:**

- Provide pre-departure counseling and re-entry support.
- Provide support with writing grant applications.
- Provide literature access and professional support in the sending country.
- Provide funds for ongoing collaborative support including ongoing mobility opportunities to remain in contact with the field for several years.
- Provide funds to continue research in the sending country.

# The Role of National and International Organizations in the Context of Graduate Studies

**Carolyn Watters**
**Dalhousie University**

## Opportunities

National and international Organizations play a pivotal role in the development and support of global networks for graduate programs and graduate student experiences. These networks and collaborations come in many forms and with many objectives, from enabling mobility of graduate students between universities to directly influencing the development of national and international policies.

The roles of the national and international organizations in this regard are intertwined and co-dependant. Norms and best practices may be developed through bottom-up as well as top-down approaches. For example, national "standards" for graduate school admission, thesis expectations, program length, etc. are mostly derived through organic bottom-up processes in which consensus is reached in practice. The recent work in the USA on Professional Master's and Professional Doctoral degrees, on the other hand, has proceeded in a more top-down fashion led by national-level working groups. International collaborations and agreements are often developed using the outcomes of both these practices. That is, national and international frameworks are developed using accepted national norms and best practices as well as models developed by "blue ribbon" panels. National frameworks can no longer, however, be viewed in isolation. The Bologna agreement, for example, is an international collaborative framework that has widespread implications outside the immediate European collaboration, including considerations of the role of the three-year bachelor degree for entrance to graduate programs in North America.

## Roles

Opportunities abound at both the national and international levels for more effective international collaboration at the graduate level. To achieve successful collaborations the context must be inclusive. That is, collaborations for graduate matters should be informed by not only universities but also by national and international organizations, governments, graduate school associations, graduate student associations, and administrative associations.

To achieve opportunities in such a context we need to develop a forum through which robust national and international agreements can be reached, and these need to:

1. Level the playing field for mobility of graduate students and graduates by setting common standards (admission, funding, program structure) and setting common expectations for students from programs and from students in programs.

2. Identify best practices in supervision, professional development, career development, and crafting international and inter-university MOUs.

3. Work with national and international institutions on the definition and recognition of joint and collaborative degrees.

4. Support coordinated policy-setting efforts at all levels of governments, including international bodies. International and national organizations often set policy for bodies that affect the lives, studies, and research of graduate students: granting agencies, research councils, student associations, graduate school associations, postdoctoral associations.

# *Best Practice Research and Outcomes Assessment*

## Lesley Wilson
## European University Association

### Introduction – Joint Degrees, "a hallmark of the European Higher Education Area"

European universities have been involved in joint programme development, in particular since the launch of the ERASMUS programme in 1988, and interest has grown rapidly, especially at the master's, but also at doctorate level with the introduction of the Bologna reforms over the last decade. Hence joint degrees have come to be seen as one of the "hallmarks of the European Higher Education Area."[1] What started as a predominantly European trend has now spilled over into international cooperation, also thanks to funding provided through the European Commission's ERASMUS Mundus programme.

The strong political pressure to increase mobility evidenced by the 20% benchmark for 2020 adopted by Ministers in the most recent Bologna Communiqué (April 2009), along with the similarly ambitious mobility targets for young researchers proposed by the European Research Advisory Board (ERAB) in its recently published vision for 2030[2] will only increase pressure to develop joint programmes and other collaborative activity as a way of promoting internationalisation and providing an organised framework within which mobility and other joint activities can take place.

### 2004 - 10 "Golden Rules" for Joint Programmes

As a preliminary survey confirmed that little information was available on joint degrees[3]—not a surprising result, also given the very recent introduction of the master's degree as a qualification in much of continental Europe—a pilot study was launched in 2003 that looked in-depth at 11 existing, i.e. already functioning, Joint master's programmes and concluded by proposing 10 "golden rules" for successful programmes. These have proved to be among the most widely used, quoted and downloaded recommendations that the association has ever published. They include very basic issues such as: know

---

1     Bologna Ministerial Communiqué, Bergen, May 2005.

2     ERAB, Preparing Europe for a new Renaissance, a strategic view of the European Research Area, October 2009.

3     EUA, Rauhvargers & Tauch, 2002.

why you are setting up the programme; choose your partners carefully; develop clear goals and student learning outcomes with partners; make sure you have institutional support, adequate academic and administrative support, and a sustainable funding strategy; ensure that information is easily accessible to students; organise and plan sufficient meetings in advance; develop a language policy and decide who is responsible for what.

The report also drew attention to a number of unresolved challenges facing institutions developing joint programmes, in particular in the areas of curriculum development, quality assurance, recognition and mobility. This led to a follow-on project that focused on detailed "how to" guidelines for institutions that were published in 2006[4] and followed up with an impact assessment two years later.

## Guidelines for Universities – Developing Best Practice

There are two main models for joint programmes, be they at master or doctoral level—even if at doctoral level the range of forms of collaboration may be broader, and structured mobility less central[5]—namely "collaborative" where the home institution awards the degree and "joint" where the candidate receives one certificate jointly awarded by the host and home university. Somewhere in between is the fuzzy situation of the double degree with the award of two certificates and the attendant problems of possible double-counting. This means that in terms of ensuring quality and developing best practice the issues that need to be tackled at institutional level are similar: "jointness" needs to be defined and a shared understanding reached, and clear decision-making mechanisms and levels of responsibility agreed, all of this to ensure fitness of purpose and fitness for purpose.

These issues form the core of the good practice guidelines developed in 2006. They are designed to help institutions through the process of establishing joint programmes from idea to concept, through the planning stage to conclusion of a joint agreement and finally to successful implementation. The guidelines concentrate on institutional decision-making and quality enhancement processes and avoid the thorny issues of external quality assurance, recognition of periods of study and of diplomas/qualifications awarded. The overall goal

---

4   EUA "Guidelines for Quality Enhancement in European Joint Masters Programmes – European Masters New Evaluation Methodology 2006"

5   There is an ongoing discussion about the pros and cons of the organization of a "European Doctorate" which until now is a form of collaboration that tends to find favour only in a small number of countries and where the question of added value remains open. Discipline differences also play a role.

was to demonstrate that successful joint degrees require a shared commitment to quality, which in turn means that the consortium as such must: discuss jointly aims and concept, agree on bottom-up self-evaluation activities at the level of each partner, undertake joint analysis of the contribution and focus of each partner and at regular intervals develop common improvement-oriented action plans covering issues such as admissions, recognition, curriculum development, access to university facilities, external evaluation procedures.

The project also concluded that the main points of substantial concern are: joint application, selection and certification; organizing, facilitating, paying for and monitoring mobility; finance and fees, especially fee differentials across partners; language policy and logistical management issues and services. Since then there is evidence to suggest that moving from the European to the international level makes sustainability concerns even more pressing thus underlining the central importance of the strength of the consortia as a whole and suggesting that even more integration in terms of both administrative and curricular issues, and development of common procedures and tools for cooperation is needed.

## Conclusions and Challenges

The guidelines developed until now have primarily addressed institutional strategies and partnership-building, looking predominantly at process and programme development issues. However as interest in joint degrees continues to grow there is an increasing need to address external factors, in particular external quality assurance and accreditation issues, but also other quality issues, which in Europe includes an increased focus on structured university networks as frameworks for cooperation.

## External Quality Assurance and Accreditation of Joint Programmes

In Europe a major priority is to try and avoid having to have joint degree curricula quality-assured by the quality agencies of each country involved in the partnership. One emerging trend is to encourage the mutual recognition of accreditation decisions taken by QA agencies in different countries, possible in some cases thanks to the growing cooperation between agencies and given the existence of a European Register of Quality Agencies (EQAR). This is more challenging at the international level but basic principles do exist, also endorsed by major university associations, and enshrined in the UNESCO/OECD Guidelines for Quality in Cross Border Education.

## Ensuring the Quality of Mobility:

Increasingly European higher education sectors/countries are developing mobility standards through Codes of Conduct for mobility that are often sector-driven and play an important role in setting the framework conditions for international students at all levels.

## Growing Importance of University Networks:

European higher education is characterised by a plethora of different university networks with different purposes and priorities. These networks have traditionally served as a framework for student mobility and are increasingly extending their activities as well as their international outreach. The trust and confidence established between the members of the network, often over years, makes them important vehicles for addressing the challenges of establishing and sustaining joint programme development at different levels. In particular with the introduction of the ERASMUS Mundus programme, member universities of these networks, working together in a "variable geometry," have been quick to establish international partnerships and also to learn that the new generation of joint programmes requires a very different approach to that of the looser partnerships of previous years.

Hence there is a trend towards tighter consortia integration both in terms of administrative issues and curriculum development. In several cases this has led to the development of common procedures and tools to facilitate cooperation among the consortium partners, thus making it easier to tackle issues such as application, selection and certification procedures, harmonizing tuition fees and to organise quality assurance and joint services. This has led to the development of joint tool kits, e.g. by the UNICA network and to the launch of specific projects looking only at network organization issues, such as the UTRECHT Network's ongoing Joint Degree Management and Administration Network (JOIMAN) that is analysing both Joint Master and Joint Doctorate programmes being implemented by the various members of the network.

It is to be expected that these trends will continue to develop with EUA, increasingly assuming an umbrella function as well as a policy and support function for many of these disciplines and other networks. The individual member universities of these networks are individual EUA members but it is interesting to note that several of the networks as such are deciding to become members of EUA or/and EUA-CDE, also in their role as networks.

# Strategic Leadership in Graduate International Collaboration

### Daniel D. Denecke
### Council of Graduate Schools

International collaborations in graduate education take a variety of forms. They take the shape of formal joint and dual degree partnerships between US institutions and partner institutions from other countries, of formal student exchanges of short duration, and of research partnerships between faculty that may or may not involve the exchange of faculty and graduate students. One of the fastest growing areas in graduate education is international joint and dual degree programs. Recent Council of Graduate Schools (CGS) survey research suggests rapid growth in formal, dual and joint degree partnerships. For example, in 2008, over half of the institutions surveyed (51%) in the largest 50 with respect to international graduate student enrollment, reported existing dual degree programs with international partner institutions, up from 41% in 2007. For all institutions, growth in dual degrees is up from 14% to 21% for all institutions during that same period (CGS 2007, 2008). Sessions devoted to this topic at CGS annual meetings and summer workshops, as well as at US regional graduate school association meetings, have resulted in the exchange of useful information about common challenges and success strategies. But graduate deans in the US have also expressed frustration in these sessions with broad confusion about: definitions and process issues, a lack of consensus on philosophical issues regarding the value of degree collaborations, and the lack of national guidelines and best practice resources to help them in their growing role of overseeing the success and quality of international degree collaborations. Through our participation in similar conversations in Europe and in Asia, we have observed that this need is now acute wherever international collaborations are valued.

While a number of useful reports and guides have appeared in the past decade on international collaborations in higher education to help decision-makers manage this growth, they have typically spoken to the European context, where such collaborations are more common and typically of longer standing. Or, where they have represented both US and European activities, they have combined both undergraduate and graduate level collaborations, and have thus proven of limited use to the US graduate community, where undergraduate degree collaborations far outnumber those at the graduate level. CGS therefore designed the Graduate International Collaborations Project, funded by a grant from the National Science Foundation, as the first step in answering the needs of graduate deans for enhanced understanding and guidance on best practices in ensuring successful collaborations, upholding institutional standards and advancing institutional goals, and maintaining the quality of the graduate experience for international and domestic students alike.

While some issues arise that are common to both undergraduate and graduate collaborations, graduate degrees, and especially research degrees, have their own distinct issues and justifications. There are also differences in the way graduate education is structured in the United States that justify a more focused US study. To better understand the US graduate perspective, CGS conducted a survey and facilitated a set of focus group discussions on both joint and dual degrees and on non-degree research collaborations. One of the overarching findings of the project thus far has been that graduate deans have moved from playing a role of primarily administrative support in such collaborations to providing: a) strategic leadership in the selection, approval, implementation and sustainability of collaborative programs, and b) core input in such collaborations when fundamental issues arise relating to the value of a graduate degree, the definition of a thesis, etc.

It is a commonplace observation in discussions of joint and dual degree programs that, given the challenges and obstacles, the most successful degree collaborations at the graduate level typically begin on the foundation of strong pre-existing faculty research collaborations. Without such a strong foundation, faculty buy-in can be difficult to achieve and top-down agreements between institutional leaders that are later proposed to each institution's respective research faculty can thus sometimes flounder. When we asked *"How are Partner Institutions typically chosen in your joint or dual degree programs?"* the majority of respondents (58.1%)[1] answered: "Known contacts among faculty/ existing faculty partnerships;" followed by "Existing partner through an already established program" (23.3%). Only 16.3 percent reported "Strategic decision to pick a new partner." Notably, at a time when some US institutions are being bombarded with offers for formal collaboration from institutions abroad, only one institution indicated that its degree collaboration was initiated by a foreign institution. However, when we asked: *"What are the primary motivations for your institution to partner with an international institution on joint and dual degree programs?,"* it was clear that strategic institutional decisions and motivations come into play at all stages while building on existing faculty collaborations or programs. The most frequently cited motivations in order of

---

1    Respondents include 43 institutions that reported on 168 programs overall.

frequency of institutional responses (out of a total of 43) were:

- Attract International Students (36)
- Faculty Interest (35)
- Strengthen Academic Research Quality (33)
- Administrative Interest in Internationalizing the Institution (33)
- Increase Prestige (22)
- Increase Revenue (19)
- Employer/Industry Demand (15)
- Other (7)
    Provide International Experience for Students (2)
    International Relations/Outreach (2)

It is in pursuing successful degree collaborations with many of these strategic institutional motivations in mind that the graduate dean has become an essential partner with faculty at every stage. In open-ended responses to a question about the role of the graduate school, several commented on the more expansive role that deans and strategic leaders have come to play not only in shepherding the process through but also in protecting student interests and advancing institutional goals. One response captures this changing role of the graduate school well:

> *Initially, it was a matter of identifying faculty linkages with colleagues overseas and then matching curricula for the degree program. These partnerships were initially based on personalism. We have worked to involve new faculty in the process through orientation, information at the opening convocation and by bringing highly qualified students from abroad to study on our campus. Exposure to exceptional students in graduate courses does a lot to convince faculty of their potential as researchers and industry leaders. Faculty begin to gravitate toward and encourage the international exchange programs.*

The role of the graduate dean in providing strategic leadership has also been important in overcoming some of the biggest challenges in establishing and maintaining joint and dual degrees. The greatest challenges identified in the Graduate International Collaborations Project survey common to both degree types with international partners identified by 50% or more of respondents were:

1. Ensuring sustainability
2. Securing adequate funding
3. Negotiating an MOU
4. Recruiting students
5. Deciding fee structure

One of the more significant challenges specific to dual degrees is the concern that they may potentially reward students with double credit for a single body of work. We asked: *Were concerns about students receiving "double credit" for a single body of work (e.g., thesis or coursework) an issue in the implementation of your international collaborative degree programs?* Responses were almost equally divided: 51% said that this was a concern, and 49% reported that this was not a concern. The double credit debate is one area where graduate deans often play an important leadership role, helping the institution to navigate administrative questions with reference to fundamental issues of value in graduate research and education. They can sometimes raise important questions like "What is a thesis?" in ways that encourage flexibility and creative thinking in an international collaboration. But they also describe themselves as challenging flexible solutions when they believe that institutional quality is being compromised.

While it would be a mistake to suggest that universities wait until the data are in from as-yet-to-be-developed, large-scale longitudinal studies of the outcomes of international collaboration before launching such degrees, one of the most important results of the CGS project has been the widespread recognition that current attempts to measure outcomes have been inadequate or non-existent. Given the resources that such programs typically require, the relative unavailability of federal and state funding to support international research collaborations in the US (as compared with many of our international partners), and the identification of sustainability and funding issues as the single greatest challenge most programs face, it is reasonable to suggest that some portion of our strategic thought be put into addressing this gap and defining and assessing measurable outcomes for all stakeholders (students, programs, institutions, and host nations). While we know the motives and objectives driving these stakeholders to participate in most international graduate collaborations, we have collectively done very little to measure progress to see whether these objectives are being met. Nationally, we have significantly more tools at our disposal to measure the outcomes of undergraduate collaborations, where a host of existing instruments quantify interaction and reflection to measure whether goals and objectives are met that typically include: identity development (self awareness and understanding), global citizenship, cultural awareness or understanding and acculturation (see, e.g., the presentations at a NAFSA 2009 Assessment session at: www. iienetwork.org/page/85022/). While these goals and motives may also be present among champions of graduate international research collaborations, the primary drivers are different and require greater national and international discussion. Beyond attitudinal changes of participating students and competencies that may be common to undergraduate international educational experiences, at the graduate level measurable outcomes may include such things as: future publication productivity (frequency, co-authorship, citations) and collaboration, the quality of research, time to degree, employment figures (breadth and level of employment), the quality of mentoring, and progress on recruitment goals. Although difficult to measure, examples of other purported benefits of collaboration would include: the contribution of diverse perspectives to the graduate community of an institution as a whole and the surrounding community; the development of in-house methodological expertise that would not have been possible without student and faculty exchange that resulted from such collaboration.

If sustainability questions continue to prove the greatest challenge to international collaborative programs, those institutions that are unable to provide answers to questions about such outcomes may find it more difficult to generate the internal and external resources necessary to ensure their viability. Just as they have risen to the challenge of joining faculty in helping to share responsibility for their initiation, approval, and development, strategic leaders in graduate education at all levels should accept a leading role in the assessment of collaborate graduate programs to the extent that such assessment is required to ensure that the goals that reflect institutional strategic priorities are being met. As first steps, strategic leaders from all countries actively engaged in international graduate collaborations should:

- help to shape national and international conversations to identify definable outcome measures, and
- integrate the assessment of programs and graduate student experiences into the assessment and review of graduate programs.

*This essay reflects the contributions of my colleagues Julia Kent, Sheila Kirby, and Nathan Bell in the Graduate International Collaborations Project. Parts of this essay were adapted from an article co-authored with Julia Kent that first appeared in the CGS Communicator (October 2009).*

## Works Cited:

Council of Graduate Schools (2010). Joint Degrees, Dual Degrees, and International Research Collaborations: A Report on the CGS International Collaborations Project.

Council of Graduate Schools (2008). 2008 Graduate Admissions Survey II: Final Applications and Initial Offers of Admissions.

Council of Graduate Schools (2007). 2007 Graduate Admissions Survey II: Final Applications and Initial Offers of Admissions.

Denecke, D. and J. Kent. (2009). The Graduate International Collaborations Project: A North American Perspective on Joint and Dual Degree Programs. *CGS Communicator* (42:8).

# The Joint IITB-Monash Ph.D.: A Model Program?

## Maxwell King
## Monash University

## Background

The Indian Institute of Technology Bombay (IITB) and Monash University have established a joint venture Research Academy based in Mumbai, India. Significant funding and support has been provided from Australian and Indian Governments and Industry. The Academy has its own CEO, Governing Board, Advisory Council, and a vehicle for joint research projects involving IITB and Monash researchers.

Initial areas of research include:

- Advanced computational engineering, simulation and manufacture
- Infrastructure engineering
- Clean energy
- Water
- Nanotechnology
- Biotechnology and stem cell research

## The Program

An important part of the Academy is the jointly awarded Ph.D. program. The framework, regulations and processes for the joint Ph.D. program took two years to develop. Many jointly awarded Ph.D. programs require the candidate to satisfy two sets of conditions—one for each institution.

We decided we wanted one program and one integrated set of requirements. We formed a Cross Institutional Program Committee (CIPC) with three representatives from each institution. This later expanded to four representatives from each university. We looked at all elements of the Ph.D. at both institutions and made decisions on requirements of the jointly awarded degree.

Recommendations were made by the CIPC on:

- Governance/administrative structure

- Admission criteria and the examination process to be followed
- Supervision/joint supervision
- Supervisory code of practise
- Conditions of candidature
- Progress seminars/complaints
- Research misconduct
- General misconduct
- Intellectual property (difficult – still a work in progress)
- Examination – nomination of examiners

A document outlining the program was approved by the Senate at IITB and Academic Board at Monash in early 2009.

One potential problem we encountered was that IITB had lower admission criteria than Monash. We addressed this issue by introducing a coursework component at IITB, which meant the admission requirements for both institutions would be met after successful completion of the coursework. There are currently 32 students enrolled in the program and the June 2009 intake involved:

- 1485 applications
- 70 interviews
- 20 offers (16 joined, 4 to join next year)

Along with the focused and timely nature of the research areas, the deep involvement of all institutions in the process of developing program policies and structures has provided a strong foundation for what promises to be a highly successful program. It is also useful to note that strong initial support from government and industry allowed the institutions involved to invest time and resources in program design before implementation. This first step will help ensure the success of the program and also help the partnering institutions avoid some of the problems that commonly arise in joint ventures.

# VII. CONCLUSION: GUIDING PRINCIPLES AND FUTURE COLLABORATION

Like the Banff and Florence summits of 2007 and 2008, the 2009 Global Summit in San Francisco produced consensus points that will be useful to university leaders in a wide variety of national contexts. These *Principles and Practices for Effective Collaborations[1]* reflect many hours of intense discussion among summit participants about the common values informing graduate international collaborations, the challenges encountered by most university leaders as they work to develop and sustain them, and practices that have proved successful for overcoming common hurdles.

Communication and collaboration is always an important goal among graduate leaders internationally, but there are two reasons why the principles approved by the summit participants are of particular importance. First, graduate leaders in many different countries are working to demonstrate the value of international graduate training to the preparation of the next generation of researchers. It is therefore crucial for these leaders to articulate shared values and goals and to share their message with both national and international stakeholders. The Preamble to the "Principles and Practices" document states this message clearly:

> *As future researchers, educators, and leaders, graduate students must be prepared to address research issues that are global in scope and to participate in research endeavors that will continue to develop across national and cultural borders. International research and educational collaborations, such as joint and dual degree programs and formal and informal research collaborations and exchanges, are key to this preparation, enabling graduate students to directly experience the challenges and opportunities of international research and education.*

Representing nine countries and six major national and international university

---

1    See Appendix A.

associations,[2] this collective statement lends formal weight to the growing recognition that international collaborations must be a key part of graduate education and research training.

The second reason that the 2009 *Principles and Practices* is of particular value is that it provides an important foundation for negotiating the many national and institutional differences that arise throughout the collaboration process. Participants developed a list of ten principles and practices for effective collaborations that will help university leaders in many countries develop a strong culture for collaboration at their own institutions and communicate effectively with current and potential partners.

While 2009 summit participants expressed enthusiasm about sharing these principles in their own countries and institutions, they also set four ambitious goals for building on these outcomes in the future. These goals include: 1) Pursuing common strategies for measuring the outcomes of international collaborations; 2) Sharing methods for communicating with institutional, national, and regional partners; 3) Using new technologies to develop virtual communities of collaboration and knowledge exchange; and 4) Developing and expanding the impact of the Global Summit. We hope that you will join us as we develop new projects and international forums that address these important areas of future work.

Debra W. Stewart
President
Council of Graduate Schools

---

2    In addition to the Council of Graduate Schools (CGS), 2009 delegates represented the Association of Chinese Graduate Schools (ACGS), the Australian Deans and Directors of Graduate Studies (DDoGS), the Canadian Association of Graduate Studies (CAGS), the European University Association (EUA), and the South Korean Council of Graduate Schools.

# APPENDIX A: PRINCIPLES AND PRACTICES OF EFFECTIVE COLLABORATIONS

The concluding session of the 2009 Strategic Leaders Global Summit was a workshop-style discussion in which participants revised and approved a set of conclusions that had received significant attention and support in earlier sessions. While the purpose of the discussion was not to reach consensus on all topics, participants agreed to a statement about the value of international collaborations, a set of principles that uphold effective collaborations, and a plan for future work.

## Preamble

As future researchers, educators, and leaders, graduate students must be prepared to address research issues that are global in scope and to participate in research endeavors that will continue to develop across national and cultural borders. International research and educational collaborations, such as joint and dual degree programs and formal and informal research collaborations and exchanges, are key to this preparation, enabling graduate students to directly experience the challenges and opportunities of international research and education. In order to ensure that such programs are effective and sustainable, however, graduate institutions must implement guiding principles and practices that take into account the benefits and requirements of all stakeholders. The participants in the 2009 Strategic Leaders Global Summit have agreed that the following principles and practices support the development of successful international collaborations between and among graduate institutions:

## Principles and Practices for Effective International Collaborations

*Effective international collaborations should*

1.  Clarify the purposes and goals of the collaboration, and the benefits to all direct stakeholders: graduate students, faculty, institution,

regions or countries affected by the collaboration.

2. Establish the rights and responsibilities of each partner before implementing collaborative activities.

3. Understand and respect different social and academic cultures, with clear agreement about points on which compromise is and is not possible.

4. Articulate and develop the roles and responsibilities of university leadership, faculty/academic staff, and students. Strong collaboration should be based on faculty or student experience and needs, within the framework of strategies articulated by university administration and/or government.

5. Develop the capacity to measure benefits, quality, and outcomes in multiple areas, including research outcomes, pedagogy, education and career training, human resources, infrastructure, and institutional finances.

6. Consider and articulate ethical standards as they pertain to different groups of stakeholders.

7. Build a dynamic institutional culture that supports international collaborations, not merely individual partnerships.

8. Ensure that the capacity exists to deliver upon commitments made to all groups of stakeholders.

9. Provide appropriate support systems for students and faculty throughout their international experience, and provide resources that help graduate students develop cultural awareness and professional skills.

10. Ensure that a record or database exists documenting past and current international collaboration agreements.

## Plan for Future Work

To ensure that the summit discussions are fostered and supported, participants also approved the following action steps:

1. Pursue common strategies for measuring outcomes, identifying common measures for Master's, PhD and professional programs while distinguishing between different metrics of success for these degree types.

2. Share methods for communicating with institutional, national, and regional partners.

3.  Use new technologies to develop virtual communities of collaboration and knowledge exchange.
4.  Develop and expand the impact of the Global Summit by developing the link between the summit and national and international policy-makers and by scaling up the event to include a broader range of regions and countries.

# APPENDIX B: PARTICIPANT BIOGRAPHIES

**Eleanor Babco** serves as Senior Consultant for the Professional Master's Program and Associate Program Director for the Professional Science Master's (PSM) project at the Council of Graduate Schools. She prepares reports and articles on the PSM project, provides information and guidance to existing PSM programs and for the development of new programs, and makes presentations addressing some aspect of the PSM. In addition, she works with the Government Relations staff and the CGS President on special projects. She is the former Executive Director of the Commission on Professionals in Science and Technology, a nonprofit corporation in Washington, DC that collects, synthesizes, analyzes and disseminates reliable information about the science and engineering workforce in the United States. She received grants from the Alfred P. Sloan Foundation, the GE Foundation, and the National Science Foundation for special studies at CPST.

Ms. Babco was educated as a chemist at Immaculata College and Catholic University, but has devoted her professional career to the analysis and interpretation of education and employment data about scientists and engineers, with particular attention to women and underrepresented minorities, and has written and published extensively on these issues. She received the WEPAN-sponsored Betty Vetter Award for Research in 2001, was named an AWIS fellow in 2002, and is a member of the Kellogg Research Council, Office for Diversity and Community Partnership, at Harvard Medical School.

**Sheila Bonde** is Dean of the Graduate School at Brown University, a post she has held since 2005. Bonde was one of the first Royce Family Professors of Teaching Excellence, and is currently Professor of History of Art and Architecture and Professor of Archaeology at Brown, where she has taught since 1984.

Dr. Bonde is PI for two projects funded by the Andrew W. Mellon Foundation: a $3 million endowment for the Mellon Graduate Fellows program, and the Mellon doctoral workshops. Bonde has also held two grants from the Council of Graduate Schools: one to develop Responsible Conduct of Research curricula in the Physical Sciences, and the other to track PhD Completion in Brown graduate programs. She is a member of the board of directors for the Council of Graduate Schools and the Association of Graduate Schools.

Dr. Bonde is an archaeologist and architectural historian. She holds a B.A. from Cornell University, and MA and PhD degrees from Harvard University. Her work on medieval monasteries and fortifications has been published in several books and numerous articles. Her excavation has been supported by US and French government grants, and her digital humanities project has been supported by the National Endowment for the Humanities.

**Jean Chambaz**, MD, received a doctorate es sciences. He is currently professor of cell biology at the Faculty of Medicine Pierre and Marie Curie and heads the department of clinical biochemistry at the hospital Pitié-Salpêtrière at Paris. He created a research unit in the field of metabolism and intestinal differentiation in 1999, which merged in 2007 into the Research Center of Cordeliers, of which he is vice-director. After heading the doctoral school in physiology and pathophysiology from 2001 to 2005, he created the Institute of Doctoral Training at UPMC which enrolls about 3500 doctoral candidates in sciences and medicine from mathematics to public health, where he served as director until October 2008. He has been elected at the scientific council and serves as vice-president for research of UPMC since 2006. He chairs the steering committee of the Council on Doctoral Education of the European University Association launched in 2008.

**Andrew C. Comrie** is Associate Vice President for Research, Dean of the Graduate College and Director of Graduate Interdisciplinary Programs at the University of Arizona. Dr. Comrie provides academic leadership for graduate education at the University, including stewardship of fourteen Graduate Interdisciplinary Programs, which involve over 600 faculty members from more than a dozen colleges. Prior to his appointment as dean in January 2006, he led the graduate program in Geography for almost a decade. Dr. Comrie has been a plenary speaker, session chair and invited participant at numerous CGS meetings on topics including interdisciplinary graduate education, strategic budgeting, admissions and financing, responsible conduct of research, entrepreneurship, master's completion and attrition, and international graduate education. He is an elected member of the CGS Board of Directors. Dr. Comrie is a climatologist with a primary appointment as Professor of Geography and with interdisciplinary appointments in Atmospheric Sciences, Arid Lands Resource Sciences, Global Change, Public Health, Remote Sensing and Spatial Analysis, and Statistics. He received his undergraduate education at the University of Cape Town in South Africa and his PhD from the Pennsylvania State University. Dr. Comrie joined the University of Arizona in 1992. Since then, he has conducted broadly interdisciplinary research in climate variability and change, with particular interests in the connections between climate and health, air quality, and environmental impacts. He continues to carry out funded research and publish, serving on several journal Editorial Boards and as Americas Editor of the International Journal of Climatology.

**Daniel D. Denecke** is Director of Best Practices at CGS. He received his PhD from the Johns Hopkins University and has served as faculty member at Georgetown University and the University of Maryland, College Park. In the best practice domain, Dr. Denecke currently serves as PI for two major CGS best practice initiatives: the Project for Scholarly Integrity (www. scholarlyintegrity.org), funded through a contract from the Office of Research Integrity to develop institutional models for embedding research ethics and the responsible conduct of research into graduate education, and the Graduate International Collaborations Project, funded by NSF to identify the facilitators and inhibitors to successful collaborative joint and dual degree programs and research projects. Prior to leading CGS efforts on these projects, Dr. Denecke directed the PhD Completion Project, Phase I, a major national initiative to address the underlying factors of students' departure from graduate study and managed the Preparing Future Faculty (PFF) program, to promote and institutionalize professional development programs for doctoral students aspiring to faculty positions. He is the lead author on a recent article on the PhD Completion Project in Doctoral Education and the Faculty of the Future (ed. Ron Ehrenberg, Cornell University Press, 2009) and has authored and co-authored synthesis publications across the range of CGS initiatives, e.g., Preparing Future Faculty in the Humanities and Social Sciences (2003) and PhD Attrition and Completion: Policy, Numbers, Leadership and Next Steps (2004).

Dr. Denecke was an early contributor to the EUA's Bologna Handbook and is regularly invited to present to international groups of higher education leaders and policymakers on international issues in graduate education such as: the implications of the Bologna Process on North American graduate admissions and university practices and mechanisms (including the creation of joint and dual degree programs) for increasing research mobility and for preparing graduate students to succeed in a global academic/research market. He has played a lead role at CGS in shaping the annual series of strategic leaders global summits on graduate education.

**Karen P. DePauw** is Vice President and Dean for Graduate Education and tenured Professor in the Departments of Sociology and Human Nutrition, Foods & Exercise at Virginia Tech in Blacksburg, Virginia. Since her arrival at Virginia Tech, her major accomplishments include success in building a strong diverse graduate community, the establishment of the innovative Graduate Life Center (GLC), and the signature initiative known as Transformative Graduate Education (TGE). As an academic administrator, she has been a strong advocate for diversity and equity in higher education and has spoken at national conferences on preparing the future professoriate and change facing the 21st century university. She has been a panelist, speaker and presenter at regional affiliates (CSGS, WAGS) and national CGS meetings and workshops. In addition, she has been an invited speaker for NSF IGERT meetings and NSF Advance conferences and workshops. She was a founding member and Facilitator/Chair for the Virginia Council of Graduate School (VCGS), served as President of the Council of Southern Graduate Schools (CSGS) 2007-2008 and currently serves as Chair of the Board of Directors of the Council of Graduate Schools (CGS).

Dr. DePauw earned the A.B. in Sociology from Whittier College, M.S. in Special Education from California State University, Long Beach, and a PhD in Kinesiology from Texas Woman's University. In the 1970s, she taught with the Los Angeles City and Los Angeles County Schools and California State University – Los Angeles before moving to Washington State University where she served 22 years on the faculty and as an administrator.

**Chaohui Du**
PhD Aerospace Engineering, Northwestern Polytechnical University, 1992
Deputy Dean of Graduate School, 2005.08-
Professor of School of Mechanical Engineering, 2002.01-
Associate Prof. and Prof of School of Power and Energy Engineering, 1998. 10-2001.12.
Visiting Scholar, University of Illinois at Urbana and Champaign, USA, 1997. 01-1998.10
Visiting Researcher, Seoul National University, South Korea, 1996. 03-1996.12
Assistant Professor, Dept of Power Machinery Engineering, 1995. 01-1996. 02
Postdoctoral Fellow University of Tokyo, Japan, 1993. 09-1995. 01
Postdoctoral Fellow, Shanghi Jiaotong University, 1992. 04-1993. 06

**Barbara Evans** is Dean of the Faculty of Graduate Studies at the University of British Columbia. As Dean she is responsible for oversight of policy, management and quality assurance for masters and doctoral programs, generic skills training and research supervision. The Faculty also provides a range of academic support and professional development programs for graduate students, supervising faculty and staff. Prior to this appointment Barbara was Pro Vice-Chancellor (Research Training) and Dean of the School of Graduate Studies (SGS) at The University of Melbourne.

Barbara has been a keynote speaker at many conferences focused on graduate education in the US, Canada, Europe, Australia and Asia. She has been the Convener of the Universitas 21 Deans and Directors of Graduate Studies and of the Australian Deans and Directors of Graduate Studies. Each group is committed to improving graduate education in a global context, quality assurance, and national and international benchmarking of research higher degree practices. Barbara is also a key member of two important global networks focused on graduate and doctoral education. One is the 'Strategic Leaders Global Summits on Graduate Education' hosted through the US Council of Graduate Schools. The other focuses on the 'Forces and Forms of Change in Doctoral Education' and is organized through the 'Center for Innovation and Research in Graduate Education' at the University of Washington.

Originally a zoologist, Barbara's research resulted in over 100 publications and she is author and editor of three award-winning Biology textbooks for tertiary and senior secondary students, each now in their fourth edition.

**Jeffery C. Gibeling** was appointed Dean of Graduate Studies at the University of California, Davis in August 2002. He oversees 87 graduate degree programs, of which more than one-half are organized as interdisciplinary graduate groups. He previously served as Chair of the Academic Senate at UC Davis and Executive Associate Dean of Graduate Studies. He joined the faculty at UC Davis as an Assistant Professor of Materials Science and Engineering in 1984. Professor Gibeling holds degrees in Mechanical Engineering and Materials Science and Engineering from Stanford University. He also worked as an Acting Assistant Professor and Senior Research Associate at Stanford from 1979 through 1984. Professor Gibeling is the author or coauthor of more than 85 publications on the mechanical properties of materials and has guided the thesis and dissertation work of 25 graduate students.

Dean Gibeling has promoted continuous improvements in information technology to enhance service of the Office of Graduate Studies to its clientele. He is also deeply committed to increasing the diversity of the graduate population at UC Davis. Under Dean Gibeling's leadership the Office of Graduate Studies has developed a comprehensive Professional Development program to ensure that graduate students complete their degrees and are prepared for successful careers. He has also devoted significant attention to the needs of postdoctoral scholars and established an award for Excellence in Postdoctoral Research. Dean Gibeling serves as Chair-elect of the CGS Board of Directors, on the Association of Graduate Schools Executive Committee and as a member of the GRE Board.

**John Hayton** was appointed Counsellor (Education) and Director of Australian Education International – North America at the Australian embassy in Washington, DC, in February 2007. John has responsibility for the bilateral education relationship with both the United States and Canada. Prior to John's appointment he directed the Americas, Europe and Multilateral Policy Section in the Australian Department of Education, Employment and Workplace Relations. John's career includes 18 years with the Australian Department of Foreign Affairs and Trade, including postings in Bangkok and New York, and three years leading and implementing an information technology industry development program in Tasmania, Australia (2001-03). When not at work John has been an active participant in community organisations including most recently as Presiding Member of the Board of the Friends School in Hobart, Tasmania and as a mentor to young men without significant male role models in their lives in Canberra, Australia. John is a Fellow of the Royal Society for the encouragement of Arts, Manufactures and Commerce.

**Chet Jablonski** completed his undergraduate studies at the University of Massachusetts, Amherst graduating *magna cum laude* as a chemistry major 1967. He then studied with E.O. Fisher (Nobel Laureate 1973) as a Fulbright student in Munich and continued in Chemistry with a stopover at the University of Colorado, Boulder and then at the University of Calgary, Alberta Canada, where he completed a PhD in Transition Metal Organometallic Chemistry in 1972. Following PDF appointments at the University of Western Ontario and Waterloo University, in 1974 he took a faculty position at Memorial University, St. John's Newfoundland, Canada. Island living, wonderful people and excellent university support contrived to develop his "Newfie" spirit and he remained in Newfoundland at Memorial University, as a professor of chemistry until 1997, publishing numerous papers in synthetic and mechanistic transition metal chemistry as well as chiral enzyme mimic catalysts, and as Associate Dean of Graduate Studies and then Dean of Graduate Studies from 1997-2007. After an unsuccessful retirement attempt to pursue salmon angling at his home on the Miramichi river in Northern New Brunswick Canada, he is now gainfully involved in both research and graduate studies in his new position as Asst.

Provost for Research and Dean of Graduate Studies at Zayed University in Dubai and Abu Dhabi, United Arab Emirates.

**Thomas Ekman Jørgensen** works for the European University Association in Brussels as responsible for the Council for Doctoral Education, covering training of researchers, structures of doctoral education, researchers' skills and doctoral education in the international perspective. Before coming to Brussels, he worked as a postdoctoral fellow at the history department of the University of Copenhagen. He received his PhD in History and Civilisation from the European University Institute in Florence, Italy.

**John Keller** is the Associate Provost for Graduate Education and Dean of the Graduate College at the University of Iowa. He received his bachelor's degree in Biology from the University of Illinois-Urbana Champaign and his master's and doctoral degrees in Biological Materials from Northwestern University. His first faculty position was at the Medical University of South Carolina in Charleston, S.C. Dr. Keller was appointed to the faculty of the College of Dentistry in 1988 and he is currently a Professor of Dental Research and Oral and Maxillofacial Surgery. He was the Director of the nationally recognized Dental Student Research Program for almost a decade. He held a Research Career Development Award from NIH and served as the Associate Director of the Comprehensive Oral Health Research Center of Discovery in Craniofacial Genetics and Anomalies in the Health Sciences Center at Iowa. Dr. Keller was elected to serve a four year term on the board of the American Division of the International Association for Dental Research and served as its President in 1997-1998. He has authored over 80 peer reviewed manuscripts and 250 abstracts pertaining to dental and orthopedic biomaterials and implant related research. Dr. Keller was appointed Associate Dean for Academic Affairs in the Graduate College in 1998. He became the interim Dean in 2000 and was appointed Associate Provost for Graduate Education and Dean of the Graduate College in May 2002. Since becoming Dean, Dr. Keller has undertaken major efforts to redistribute resources to graduate students and programs using student and program outcome measures. He led efforts to establish a uniform tuition remission program at Iowa and he has aided in the establishment of several new and expanded graduate fellowship programs. He has also provided oversight for the development of over twelve new graduate programs at Iowa since 2000, as well as the initiation of the Office of Graduate Ethnic Inclusion, designed to coordinate diversity efforts at the graduate level. In 2007, the Graduate College and the University of Iowa was named one of the "Best

Places to Work" for postdoctoral scholars by *The Scientist*. Dr. Keller has made a number of presentations at regional and national workshops, including expansion of diversity efforts and resource allocations at the graduate level. He has served on national graduate committees in the Association of Graduate Schools and the Council of Graduate Schools. Most recently, he completed a two year term as Chair of the Committee on Institutional Cooperation graduate deans group, before being elected to serve on the board of directors for the AGS and CGS.

**Julia D. Kent** has been Program Manager in the Best Practices division at the Council of Graduate Schools since October 2008. She received her graduate training at Johns Hopkins University (PhD 2007), the Université de Paris VII (Maîtrise 2000), and the École Normale Supérieure, Ulm (1997-99). Before arriving at CGS, she was Assistant Professor at the American University of Beirut, where she served on the Executive Committee of the Center for American Studies and Research and helped to develop an American Studies program and research center that draws visiting scholars from North America, Europe, and the Middle East. At CGS, Dr. Kent conducts research for the Graduate International Collaborations Project, an NSF-funded project focusing on the development and implementation of joint and dual degree programs and research exchanges, and the Project for Scholarly Integrity (PSI). She also manages the Strategic Leaders Global Summit and is editor of *Global Perspectives on Research Ethics and Scholarly Integrity* (CGS 2009) and the current volume.

**Hasuck Kim** is currently a Professor of Chemistry at the Seoul National University. He received his BS from the Seoul National University, MS and PhD from the University of Illinois at Urbana-Champaign. He spent 2 years at the University of Florida as a research associate. He, then, was appointed as an Assistant Professor in 1977 at SNU where he is currently a full Professor since 1987. He spent a year at the Division of Chemistry and Chemical Engineering, California Institute of Technology as a visiting associate in 1988. He was the Dean of College of Natural Sciences, SNU from 2002 to 2004. He served as a vice president of the International Society of Electrochemistry for 3 years from 2002. His current research interests are development of electroanalytical methods based on molecular recognition and molecular switching, and electrochemistry for fuel cells. He is currently serving as the Vice President and Dean of Graduate School at SNU. Also, he is the President of the Society of International Gifted in Science since 2006, President of the Korea National

Research Resources Center. As for editorial services, he is a regional editor of Fuel Cells and editorial board member of Journal of Electroanalytical Chemistry and Analytical Sciences. He was awarded the Q. Won Choi Prize, Korean Chemical Society in 2003, Outstanding Achievements in Natural Science from Metropolitan Seoul City in 2008. He is a Fellow of International Society of Electrochemistry and a fellow member of the Korean Academy of Science and Technology in Natural Sciences.

**Maxwell King** is internationally recognised as a distinguished researcher in the field of econometrics. He has been a professor at Monash University since 1986. He is currently Pro Vice-Chancellor (Research and Research Training) and was appointed as a Sir John Monash Distinguished professor in 2003. He was head of the department of Econometrics and Business Statistics from 1988 to 2000. Professor King was made a Fellow of the Academy of Social Sciences in 1997 and a Fellow of the Journal of Econometrics in 1989. He has held visiting professorships at the University of Auckland and the University of California, San Diego. He is a founding member of the Australian Council of Deans and Directors of Graduate Studies and is currently the Council's Convenor. Despite a significant administrative load, he remains an active researcher having published over 100 journal articles. He has supervised 41 PhD students to completion and received the Vice-Chancellor's award for postgraduate supervision in 1996.

**Philip J. Langlais** is Vice President for Graduate Studies and Research at Old Dominion University and holds degrees from Northeastern University, the University of Texas Medical Branch, and Salem State College. He is a strong advocate for institutional commitment to diversity, inclusivity, ethics, multidisciplinary and global perspectives for higher education. He has spoken at national and international conferences on the need for ethics and RCR training and on the role of the graduate dean in creating the culture and reward system that will place these programs firmly within the curriculum. Dr. Langlais is a founding member of the Virginia Council of Graduate Schools, past President of the Conference of Southern Graduate School, and member of the CGS Board of Directors, He has been a panelist, speaker and presenter at regional affiliates (CSGS) and national CGS meetings and workshops. Among his major accomplishments at ODU are a two tiered institutional training and assessment program in ethics, professional standards and responsible conduct, expansion of study abroad and international research and academic collaborations, the development of a graduate management information system, a graduate enrollment tracking and projection system, establishment of an administrative and academic structure for interdisciplinary programs and the development of a comprehensive strategic plan for increasing doctoral quality and productivity. Dr. Langlais is a neuroscientist whose animal model and human research has focused on the role and mechanisms of vitamin B1 deficiency and alcohol abuse in cognitive and memory disturbances.

**Helene Marsh** has been Dean of Graduate Research Studies at James Cook University (JCU) since 1997 and is a member of the Executive and Convenor-Elect of the Australian Council for Deans and Directors of Graduate Study. More than 30% of the doctoral students at JCU are international students; many are from developing countries reflecting the university's tropical location, expertise and strategic intent: a brighter future for the tropics worldwide through education and research. A significant proportion of doctoral students at JCU are enrolled in joint degrees with international universities. Helene has been a member of the Forces and Forms Taskforce in Doctoral Education formed by the Centre for Innovation and Research in Graduate Education at the University of Washington and has recently co-authored a book chapter entitled 'Promising policies and practices for doctoral education for a global knowledge society.' Helene's substantive position is Professor of Environmental Science at JCU and she has been on the Committees of more than 50 doctoral and 20 Master's candidates. Helene has received several international awards for her interdisciplinary research on marine mammal conservation.

**Jim McGinty** was named Vice Chairman of Cambridge Information Group (CIG) in November 2004, after serving as President since February of 2000. As Vice Chairman, Jim along with Bob Snyder is responsible for the strategic direction of all CIG companies. Jim moved to CIG from CSA (now ProQuest), where he was President from 1992 to 2000. During Jim's tenure, CSA experienced a three-fold growth in revenue, and its customer base increased by 1200 institutions in over 30 countries. Prior to joining CSA, Jim spent over 20 years with Dun & Bradstreet. His last assignment was Managing Director D&B North Pacific Business Information Group based in Hong Kong. Jim's prior assignments at D&B included VP National Accounts, VP Market Management, and VP Group Government Marketing with corporate wide marketing and R&D responsibilities in the Federal sector. Jim has served on the Board of Directors of the Information Industry Association (IIA) and NFAIS. Currently, he is a Board member of CIG, ProQuest, Sotheby's Institute of Art and MarketResearch.com. Jim holds a B.A. and M.B.A. from

St. John's University in New York and received an Honorary Doctorate from his alma mater in 1984. Subsequent to graduating from St. John's, Jim was commissioned as a Marine Officer and served in Vietnam. He spent 21 years in the Marine Corps Reserve, retiring as a Colonel. He and his wife Pat reside in Vienna, VA and have three grown children, Clete, Kyle and Devin.

**Austin McLean** is the Director of Scholarly Communication and Dissertation Publishing for ProQuest, Ann Arbor, Michigan, and is responsible for the staff that develops and manages the Dissertations and Master's Theses products in all formats (electronic, print, microfilm) under the UMI and ProQuest brands. Austin is a frequent speaker at library conferences, having delivered presentations at ALA, Online Information, LIBER, and ETD among others. He serves at Treasurer of the Networked Digital Library of Theses and Dissertations (NDLTD), a non-profit group dedicated to sharing knowledge and best practices for Electronic Theses and Dissertations (ETDs).

**Kyung Chan Min**

| | |
|---|---|
| 1-1981 | PhD Mathematics Carleton University, Canada |
| 2008-present | Dean of Graduate School Yonsei, University Korea |
| 2002-2005 | Dean of University College Yonsei, University Korea |
| 2008-present | Member, Presidential Advisory Council on Education, Science and Technology of Korea |
| 2008-present | Chairman, Policy Advisory Committee, Ministry of Education, Science and Technology of Korea |
| 2008-present | President, Citizen's Coalition of Scientific Society |
| 2006-2008 | Chairman, Council for Promotion of Basic Sciences Research, National Sciences & Technology Council of Korea |
| 2005-2006 | President, Korean Mathematical Society (KMS) |
| 2003-2005 | President, Korea Association of Liberal Educations |

**Patrick S. Osmer** is Vice Provost for Graduate Studies and Dean of the Graduate School at The Ohio State University. Appointed in 2006, Osmer has since engaged Ohio State's graduate community in several major efforts, including a comprehensive assessment of the quality of Ohio State's 91 doctoral programs. The report categorizes Ohio State's doctoral programs as ranging from high-quality to those that are disinvestment candidates. The assessment process also uncovered a need for Ohio State to assess its wide-ranging life and environmental science efforts and Osmer is co-chairing two task forces to determine how Ohio State can best move forward in these areas.

Osmer is an authority on distant quasar evolution. He joined Ohio State as professor and chair of the department of astronomy in 1993. During 13 years as chair, Osmer provided leadership for building the department to internationally recognized high levels. In 2004, he was named Distinguished Professor of Mathematical and Physical Sciences.

Osmer came to Ohio State from Tucson's National Optical Astronomy Observatory where he had been deputy director from 1988-1993. From 1969-1986, Osmer was on the staff of the Cerro Tololo Inter-American Observatory in La Serena, Chile. He served as director from 1981-1985. Osmer earned a B.S. in astronomy with highest honors from the Case Institute of Technology and a PhD in astronomy from the California Institute of Technology.

**Douglas Peers** has been Professor of History and Dean of the Faculty of Graduate Studies and Associate Vice-President (Graduate) at York University, since 2007. Previously he was Interim Dean and Associate Dean (Research and Development), Faculty of Social Sciences at the University of Calgary. In 2004 he served as interim Vice-President (Programs Branch) of the Social Sciences and Humanities Research Council of Canada. From 1996 to 2005 he sat on the Board of Directors of the Shastri Indo-Canadian Institute, and from 2005 to the present he has been an executive member of Aid to Scholarly Publications Program of the Canadian Federation for the Humanities and Social Sciences. He has also served as a member of the Board of the Alberta Gaming Research Institute. Currently, Douglas Peers is Vice-President/President-elect of the Canadian Association for Graduate Studies and is a member of the Council of Ontario Universities Quality Assurance Transition/Implementation Task Force.

He is the author of Between Mars and Mammon: Colonial Armies and the Garrison State in Early-Nineteenth Century India (1995), India Under Colonial Rule, 1700-1885 (2006), as well as articles on the intellectual, political, medical and literary legacies of colonial rule in India in such journals as Social History of Medicine, Modern Asian Studies, Canadian Journal of History, Journal of Imperial and Commonwealth History, International History Review and Journal of World History. With Nandini Gooptu, he is currently co-editing India and the British Empire, a companion volume in the Oxford History of the British Empire series.

**Mary Ritter** was appointed Pro-Rector for Postgraduate Affairs at Imperial College London in October 2004, and added the International portfolio in October 2005. She was Head of the Department of Immunology from 2004-

2006, and from 1999 to February 2006 was Director of the Graduate School of Life Sciences and Medicine (GSLSM) at Imperial.

After a BA in Zoology and DPhil in Immunology from the University of Oxford, and Research Fellowships at the University of Connecticut, USA and Imperial Cancer Research Fund, London UK, she took up an academic post at the Royal Postgraduate Medical School – now the Hammersmith Campus of Imperial College London, following the 1997 merger. Her research programme centres on the development of the immune system, and she has published more than 100 peer-reviewed articles on her research. She has supervised more than 20 PhD students, all of whom have successfully gained their degree.

She was the founding Director of the GSLSM at Imperial College, steering the Graduate School through from inception in 1999 to its current overarching role providing interdisciplinary research activities, an extensive skills training programme and quality assurance for all the postgraduate students in the Faculty of Natural Sciences (Life Sciences Divisions) and Faculty of Medicine. She subsequently helped to establish Imperial's second Graduate School, of Engineering and Physical Sciences, launched in 2002. She initiated and oversees both the design and delivery of Imperial College's postgraduate and postdoctoral transferable skills training programme. In addition, she has established new academic taught courses at both bachelor's and master's level and regularly teaches undergraduate and postgraduate students in her specialist area of immunology as well as running workshops in transferable skills. She is Chair of Imperial's 'Bologna Task Force.'

She sits on a number of national and international committees including the UK Medical Research Council's Non-Clinical Careers Training and Development Panel, the UK Prime Minister's Initiative (PMI) 2 for Higher Education, The Academy of Medical Sciences' Academic Careers Committee (non-clinical), the European Universities Association (EUA) Institutional Evaluation Programme Panel of Experts, the German Excellence Initiative (Institutional Strategies) Evaluation Group, and the Programme Review Committee for the Cambridge-MIT Institute. She chairs the UK Research Councils' "VITAE" (previously UK GRAD) National Advisory Board and the UKIERI Evaluation Panel, is Vice Chair of the Steering Committee of the EUA Council on Doctoral Education, and has been a member of external evaluation and review panels for universities in Finland, Germany, France and Portugal.

**Dorris R. Robinson-Gardner** has served the higher education community for more than thirty-nine years. She has served at public, private, two-year, and four-year colleges and universities earning tenure and promotion as an assistant professor, associate professor and professor.

She holds degrees from Arkansas Baptist College and Ouachita Baptist University where she was Phi Delta Kappa and Alpha Epsilon Lambda. She received her PhD in higher education from the University of Arkansas at Fayetteville and was among the first African-Americans to receive this degree. She has been a Fulbright Scholar to China, and Korea, lectured nationally and internationally including Germany, France, and Cuba, served as a reviewer for federal agencies including the National Science Foundation, National Institutes of Health, several publishing companies and consultant evaluator for the Southern Association of Colleges and Universities.

In 1997, she became Dean of the Graduate School at Jackson State University. Under her administration, graduate enrollment increased by 80%, retention rates climbed to 82% and the graduation rate increased to 79%. She provided leadership in assisting JSU in obtaining the Carnegie Commission classification as a doctoral research-intensive university and reclassification as a research university, high research activity. She developed CyberOrientation and CyberAdvising providing graduate students with access to on-line orientation and advising and a series on Best Practices in Graduate Education.

Dr. Gardner is President of the Council of Historically Black Graduate Schools (CHBGS), serves on the Board of the Conference of Southern Graduate Schools (CSGS) and was recently elected to the Board of Directors of the Council of Graduate Schools (CGS) in Washington DC. She is married and has four children and three grandchildren.

**William B. Russel** has been dean of the Graduate School at Princeton University since 2002, the administrative home of more than 2,500 graduate students pursuing Master's and doctoral degrees. The Graduate School supports 41 departments and programs in all aspects of the endeavor from recruiting though graduate alumni relations, including both academic and student life responsibilities. He is also the A.W. Marks '19 Professor in the Department of Chemical Engineering, having joined the Princeton faculty in 1974, and continues to pursuer research that includes the theory and fabrication of micro-patterns in thin polymer films, the drying and cracking of paint films, and the behavior of colloidal gels. He is the author or coauthor of two books, the *Dynamics of Colloidal Systems* and *Colloidal Dispersions* and received the American Chemical Society's "2007 Award in Colloid and Surface Chemistry."

After receiving his B.A and M.Ch.E degrees from Rice University and a PhD from Stanford, he held a NATO Postdoctoral Fellowship in the

Department of Applied Mathematics and Theoretical Physics at Cambridge University. At Princeton he has served as chairman of Department of Chemical Engineering and director of the Princeton Materials Institute. Dean Russell is a member of the National Academy of Engineering and the American Academy of Arts and Sciences, and currently serves as past-chair of the board of the Council of Graduate Schools, a member of the board of trustees of the Bermuda Institute of Ocean Sciences, and member of the A*STAR Graduate Academy International Advisory Panel.

**Allison Sekuler** is the Canada Research Chair in Cognitive Neuroscience, Professor of Psychology, Neuroscience and Behaviour, and Associate Vice-President and Dean (Graduate Studies) at McMaster University. She received her B.A. in Mathematics and Psychology from Pomona College in 1986, and her PhD in Psychology from the University of California, Berkeley in 1991.

In her current and previous administrative positions, Dr. Sekuler developed initiatives to support and enhance graduate student life and research training, spearheaded the development of new undergraduate research initiatives, created new programs for Postdoctoral Research Fellows, and facilitated the development of innovative international and interdisciplinary partnerships for research and graduate studies.

Dr. Sekuler's research focuses on vision science, cognitive neuroscience, aging, and neural plasticity. She has won numerous national and international awards for research, teaching and leadership, and has served on and chaired provincial, federal, and international panels and external boards related both to her research and to McMaster's mission.

Dr. Sekuler is deeply committed to knowledge translation, co-founding several public outreach programs, including Science in the City, the MACafé Scientifique, and the Innovation Café, an helping create the national Canadian Institutes for Health Research Café Scientifique series. Dr. Sekuler served as President of the Royal Canadian Institute for the advancement of science from 1998-2000 (council member, 1994-2002). She is a frequent public lecturer and commentator on scientific and research issues in the national and international media, and she currently serves on the national steering committee for the Science Media Centre of Canada.

**Debra W. Stewart** became the fifth President of the Council of Graduate Schools in July 2000. Previously she was Vice Chancellor and Dean of the Graduate School at North Carolina State University. Other leadership positions include Interim Chancellor at UNC-Greensboro (1994) and Graduate Dean

(1988-95) and Vice Provost and Dean (1995-98) at NC State. She holds degrees from Marquette University (BA, philosophy), University of Maryland (MA, Government) and the University of North Carolina, Chapel Hill (PhD, Political Science).

Stewart's service to graduate education includes chairing the Graduate Record Examination Board, the Council on Research Policy and Graduate Education, the Board of Directors of Oak Ridge Associated Universities, and the Board of Directors of CGS. She also served as vice chair of the ETS Board of Trustees, Trustee of the Triangle Center for Advanced Studies, and member of the American Council on Education Board and several National Research Council Committees, as well as on advisory board for the Carnegie Initiative on the Doctorate, the Responsive PhD Proejct, and the Task Force on Immigration and America's Future. In November 2007, her leadership in graduate education was recognized by the Universite Pierre et Marie Curie with an honorary doctorate. Her alma mater, the University of North Carolina Chapel Hill honored her in October 2008 with the Distinguished Alumna Award.

Stewart is author, coauthor, and editor of books and numerous scholarly articles on administrative theory and public policy. Her research focuses on ethics in managerial decision-making.

**Susan Stites-Doe** is the Dean of Graduate Studies and a Professor at the College at Brockport, State University of New York. Dr. Stites-Doe has served as Graduate Dean at The College at Brockport for seven years, where graduate enrollments average 1400 students a semester, across 20 graduate departments. Dr. Stites-Doe serves on the Council of Graduate Schools Board of Directors, on the Graduate Record Exam (GRE) Board, and on the Test of English as a Foreign Language (TOEFL) Board.

Dr. Stites-Doe serves as the chair of the campus Professional Science Masters (PSM) Advisory Council, and coordinates interaction with external board of advisor members including representatives from Bausch and Lomb, Kodak, Vaccinex, Mercer, Novamer, and Medingen. Brockport's single PSM program in Biological Sciences will be joined by other new programs in the near future.

In 2006/2007 Dr. Stites-Doe was awarded a two-part Fulbright Senior Specialist Fellowship to work at Debrecen University in Hungary, which is developing Masters Programs following Hungary's adoption of the Bologna declaration in 1999. Since 2005 she travels to Singapore to teach in an Executive MBA program in Singapore.

Dr. Stites-Doe holds a full professorship in the Business Administration department, where she has been recognized with a Chancellor's Award for Excellence in Teaching. In 1999 she served as Faculty in Residence at Eastman Kodak and Company, where she worked with the Director of Diversity Management to conduct a benchmarking and best practice study on strategic diversity initiatives. Her journal publications feature topics such as leadership and CEO compensation.

**Dick Strugnell** assumed the role of Pro Vice-Chancellor (Graduate Research) at the University of Melbourne in December 2007. As Pro Vice-Chancellor (Graduate Research), Professor Strugnell has responsibility for activity performance, oversight of the support mechanisms and academic extension programs, and quality assurance of research higher degrees at The University of Melbourne.

Professor Strugnell is also Head of the Melbourne School of Graduate Research (MSGR). The School has an integral role within the University's research environment, offering a range of enrichment activities and support mechanisms that contribute to the success of the University's graduate research candidates as well as the administration of the Research Higher Degree.

Professor Strugnell holds a Bachelor of Science degree with Honours and was awarded his Doctorate of Philosophy from Monash University. He is a medical microbiologist with an interest in vaccines against bacterial infections and anti-bacterial immune responses. He has worked at Monash University, the University of Birmingham and the Wellcome Research Laboratories in the United Kingdom.

Professor Strugnell's interest in graduate training grew from his supervisory experience and his work in the CRC for Vaccine Technology where he was part of the Education Advisory Committee, a body that provided great extension opportunities, including IP training and funded work experience, to some 90 PhD students over 13 years. He joined the Postgraduate Scholarships Committee and then the School of Graduate Studies as an Associate Dean at the University of Melbourne in 2005.

Professor Strugnell has published more than 120 peer-reviewed papers and his research is currently funded by the NHMRC, the ARC and the Gates Foundation. He has served on NHMRC Grant Review Panels, and is currently Panel Selector for Microbiology with the NHMRC.

**Carolyn Watters** (BSc, MSc, MLS, PhD) is the President of the Canadian Association for Graduate Studies (CAGS) for the year 2009. CAGS is the national organization representing graduate education institutions on graduate student issues in Canada. Carolyn is also a Professor in the Faculty of Computer Science and the Dean of the Faculty of Graduate Studies at Dalhousie University in Halifax, Nova Scotia. As part of her outreach agenda on issues related to graduate and postdoctoral studies she produces regularly the Deans Blog and Deans Podcast series, which focus attention on current topics to a wide national and international audience.

**Lesley Wilson** joined EUA at its creation in 2001 and formally took over as Secretary General in 2002. Previous to this, she held a number of senior positions in higher education and research management at European level, in particular as Director of UNESCO's European Centre for Higher Education in Bucharest (UNESCO-CEPES) from 1995 to late 1999, Head of the newly established Science Policy Unit at the European Science Foundation in Strasbourg (1994/1995) and Director of the EC TEMPUS Office in Brussels from 1990 to 1994. A graduate of the University of Glasgow and the Institut des Hautes Etudes Européennes at the University of Strasbourg, she spent her early career as a scientific staff member of the German Science Council in Cologne before moving to Brussels in 1988 to join the newly established ERASMUS Bureau.